# THE PERSONAL, PRIVATE, PROFESSIONAL, POLITICAL LIFE AND LEGACY OF THE HONORABLE SHIRLEY ANITA ST. HILL CHISHOLM-HARDWICK

Shirley Chisholm lived most of her life in secrecy and made a special effort to protect herself from the public, especially her personal and private life. She lived a very painful and lonely life surrounded by few friends and family.

When Congresswoman Chisholm retired as a politician in 1983, she completely removed herself from political life. Hundreds of mass media people, film writers, book publishing companies, producers and authors have sought information about her personal and private life. Many of them offered $25,000 to $50,000 for this information.

## DR. WILLIE JAMES GREER KIMMONS

authorHOUSE®

*AuthorHouse™*
*1663 Liberty Drive*
*Bloomington, IN 47403*
*www.authorhouse.com*
*Phone: 833-262-8899*

*Published by AuthorHouse 09/14/2022*

*ISBN: 978-1-6655-6928-6 (sc)*
*ISBN: 978-1-6655-7041-1 (e)*

# TABLE OF CONTENTS

# DEDICATION

A Brief Narrative of the Life and Legacy of Mrs.
Shirley Anita St. Hill Chisholm-Hardwick

After years of discussions, my adopted godmother, the Honorable Shirley Chisholm, asked me to write about her life. She encountered tremendous issues while growing up in the Brooklyn, New York/Bedford -Stuyvesant community and on the island of Barbados. A number of people have written excerpts of Mrs. Chisholm's life as a public figure even though these writers spent very little if any quality time with her. This is one of the main reasons she asked me to write this narrative. It contains some of the crucial elements of her life that had a profound impact on developing the kind of person she became. As her adopted godson, I am honored and pleased to dedicate this narrative about "Mrs. C", as I called her, a giant of a woman who inspired Black, brown and white women that had an interest in entering the political arena.

I had the opportunity to spend many hours in her homes in Palm Coast, Florida and Ormond Beach, Florida from 1992 to 2004 and my home in Daytona Beach, Florida before her untimely death January1, 2005. We discussed and proofread the many drafts of this document. I'm indebted to her for the heartfelt confidence and trust she had in me to reveal the events she experienced while growing up. She knew I would not divulge any of the information we discussed during our, political, educational and teachable moments until she passed away.

Mrs. Chisholm's career in politics started in the early 1950's at the lowest rung on the political ladder in what was known as the all-male Brooklyn's boss-run Democratic Clubhouses. She became extremely persistent in challenging the inequities and injustices of the male dominated political machine. Mrs. Chisholm was quickly regarded as a woman who didn't "know her place" and a trouble-maker who had to be reckoned with. She was labeled as a little Black woman who had too much mouth and seriously needed to be dealt with. Throughout her political career and life, she received numerous death threats from people of all colors, mostly males.

Mrs. Chisholm never deviated from her life and political goals in spite of these threats. She often stated that her enemies had no particular color or gender, God was her protector.

So, she persevered and endured and became extremely successful as a dynamic fighting Black woman. She always believed in her own life's purpose. Her grandmother, Emaline Seale, in Barbados taught her to put the needs of her people before political expediency.

Mrs. Chisholm had a tremendous life as an educator, community leader, public servant, author, politician and women's rights activist. Most of this has been noted and documented in the media, newspapers, magazines, radio, television, the internet, interviews and books. This is an indication of this remarkable woman and her contributions to this country and especially to Black, brown and white women.

This brief narrative addresses her political accomplishments in addition to focusing on her personal and private life before and after her retirement from politics in 1983. As her adopted godson, I called Mrs. Chisholm "Mrs. C." I was the child she never birthed. Our relationship lasted from the time I was in third grade until she died in 2005. Shirley Chisholm lived 22 special and productive years after her retirement from politics, most of those years in Florida, Palm Coast and later Ormond Beach.

This book documents the many events she would not share as a public, political person. As her adopted godson, she personally said to me, "Willie, if I die before you, I want you to reveal another side of Shirley Anita St. Hill Chisholm-Hardwick that most people have not witnessed or read about." After retiring as a college president, I moved to Daytona Beach, Florida near my adopted godmother in Ormond Beach, Florida. We spent 3 to 5 days a week together discussing at length the true and real side of Shirley Chisholm that she protected from her estranged family and the public.

I am pleased to dedicate this narrative to Mrs. Chisholm's life and legacy and to the Black, brown and white women whom she politically inspired. I'm personally devoted to this courageous Black female. Fighting Shirley was a tiny, Black woman who spoke with a huge voice.

*Dr. Willie J. Greer Kimmons, adopted godson of the Honorable*
*Shirley Anita St. Hill Chisholm-Hardwick*

# ACKNOWLEDGEMENTS

This narrative represents the tireless efforts, collaborations and the invaluable support of numerous people who proof-read the many drafts of this manuscript. Thanks to the number of researchers and friends of Mrs. Chisholm who granted me permission to cite their personal and working relationship with her. This narrative project grew out of the vast knowledge and experience of Mrs. Shirley Chisholm throughout her life as a public servant, community leader and elected political official. This project was born for the many Black and brown females who are striving to hold political offices at the local, regional, state and national levels. It was also written because of the many struggles Black and brown women endured in life trying to be respected and appreciated as valuable human beings. This narrative will acknowledge their outstanding contributions to this country and the world. Thank God for the likes of Harriet Tubman, Sojourner Truth, Dr. Mary McLeod Bethune, Fannie Lou Hammer, Dorothy Height and, of course, the Honorable Shirley Chisholm and many more powerful Black and brown women.

Dr. Willie J. Greer Kimmons
Daytona Beach, Florida
November 30, 2022

# FOREWORD

As a lawyer, motivational speaker, radio personality, writer and President/CEO of The National Congress of Black Women, Inc., I realize the importance of the "Life and Legacy of Mrs. Shirley Chisholm." She was the first chairperson of the NCBW. Inc. organization in 1984. This historical perspective is a must read for all women and men, young and old, especially Black and brown women. The narrative is quite appropriate, fitting and timely as we witness white, Black and brown women making strides in the political arenas. Women are gaining grounds as school board and city council members, state representatives, senators, attorneys general and governors; also, United States Congresswomen, senators, vice president and now, judges. The most prominent being Justice Ketanji Brown Jackson, the first Black woman on the U.S. Supreme Court.

This documentation cites many challenges, racial and sexual concerns, and other difficult circumstances in a predominately white male political landscape. The narrative can be used as an educational and political resource for all women who are pursuing a political future at the local, regional, state and national levels. It should be required reading for history, political science and education departments at high schools, two- and four-year colleges and universities. Including sororities, fraternities, especially Black sororities, Black churches, Black, brown and white women's groups and organizations. This narrative serves as a source of information on how to survive in a racist, sexist and political environment. I encourage all interested business leaders, educators, political leaders, students, community leaders and concerned women-- especially Black and brown women-- to read this very important narrative. I am delighted to write the foreword to this excellent display of the Honorable Shirley Chisholm's personal, private, professional and political life.

With warm regards,

Dr. E. Faye Williams, MPA, DPA, D. Min, D. Th, Esq.
President/CEO, National Congress of Black Women, Inc.
Washington, D.C., November 30, 2022

# PREFACE

I am Dr. Bishop Richard G. Clark, senior Pastor of Ebenezer Missionary Baptist Church in Memphis, Tennessee since September 1997. As a religious leader in the Memphis community and a successful businessman, I have been asked to write the Preface for the book outlining the tremendous contributions of a history maker, the Honorable Congresswoman Shirley Chisholm. Mrs. Chisholm's godson, Dr. Willie J. Greer Kimmons is the author of the book and a lifelong member of Ebenezer Missionary Baptist Church since 1953.

We should always remember the outstanding political contributions that Congresswoman Shirley Chisholm made for Black, white and brown women in this country. Mrs. Chisholm laid the ground work and made it possible for Barack Obama, Hillary Clinton, Kamala Harris and Kentanji Brown Jackson to have the vision to seek the office of Vice President and President of the United States and Supreme Court Judge. The Honorable Shirley Chisholm was the first African American woman to be elected to the U.S. Congress in 1968. As an eager, astute fighter and trail blazer, she was the first Black female to seek the office of the presidency of the United States for a major political party in 1972.

As a young religious leader and truly a man of God, I am proud and honored to write the <u>Preface</u> for the book written by Mrs. Chisholm's godson, Dr. Willie J. Greer Kimmons. The title of the book is <u>The Personal, Private, Professional, Political Life and Legacy of the Honorable Shirley Anita St. Hill Chisholm-Hardwick.</u> The book is a tremendous asset and contribution documenting the life and legacy of an outstanding human being, public and political servant for all people, especially women. I strongly recommend everyone to make a concerted effort to read this great book and share it with our educators, people of goodwill and our children, grandchildren and great grandchildren.

Dr. Bishop Richard G. Clark, Senior Pastor
Ebenezer Missionary Baptist Church
Memphis, Tennessee
June 8, 2022

# DR. WILLIE J. KIMMONS
*Biography*

Motivational Speaker

Author

Educator

Administrator

Military Officer

Parent/Grandparent

Health Spokesperson

Community Activist

Humanitarian

"A STRONG VOICE FOR OUR
CHILDREN, PARENTS AND TEACHERS"

**Dr. Willie J. Kimmons** was born in Hernando, Mississippi. He was raised in Memphis, Tennessee where he attended public schools and received his high school diploma from Frederick Douglass High School. He was a student athlete and received an athletic scholarship to attend Lincoln University in Jefferson City, Missouri. While at Lincoln University, he was active in the Student Government Association and ROTC. He served as First Lieutenant in the United States Army, Adjutant General Corps, during the Vietnam era as an administrative, data processing, and personnel officer. Dr. Kimmons is a life-long member of Kappa Alpha Psi Fraternity, 1964.

**Dr. Kimmons** received his undergraduate education at Lincoln University in Jefferson City, Missouri, in Health Education and Psychology. He received his Master's Degree in Curriculum and Instruction and his Doctorate Degree in Educational Administration and Supervision in Higher Education at the age of 28 from Northern Illinois University in DeKalb, Illinois.

**Dr. Kimmons** has served at every level in the higher education teaching and learning process with dedication and distinction. Over the past forty years, he has been a Classroom Teacher; superintendent of schools; a College Professor; College President and College Chancellor.

Currently he is serving as an Educational Consultant for Pre-K-16 schools, author and as a Motivational/Empowerment speaker. Dr. Kimmons also serves as consultant in the areas of Title I programs; parental involvement; teacher and administrative training. He provides consultant services for public and private schools, two and four-year colleges and universities throughout the country. He is one of America's leading authorities on education, leadership, parental involvement, and health related issues. He is a nationally recognized consultant, speaker, seminar leader, and author of seven (7) books.

**Dr. Kimmons** made his <u>first</u> of many presentations at the National Alliance of Black School Educators Conference in Miami, Florida in <u>1974.</u> He has given more than 500 presentations and lectures to a variety of organizations including: educational associations; Chambers of Commerce; elementary, middle, and high schools; 2 year colleges, 4 year colleges, and universities; churches and other religious organizations; Kiwanis; Rotary; Lions; NAACP; Urban League; economic development organizations; political groups; Greek organizations; youth groups; parenting groups; daycare centers; Head Start programs; civic and other community organizations.

**Dr. Kimmons** for over 30 years served as a health care advocate. He is a national spokesperson and proposal reviewer for diabetes, breast and prostate cancers, and health related matters and he serves on the African American Men's Health Summit, Steering Committee for Central Florida.

He is a member of the Volusia and Flagler Counties African American Men's Prostate Cancer Board of Directors, Daytona Beach, Florida.

**Dr. Kimmons** is Vice-Chairperson of the Daytona Beach Community Relations Council; Vice-Chairperson of Daytona Beach/Volusia County Association for Retarded Citizens; Board member of Daytona Beach/Volusia County Health Department; Vice President of the Volusia County Florida Men Against Destruction-Defending Against Drugs and Social Disorder, (MAD DADS); Facilitator of "Young Male's Rites of Passage Program", Greater Friendship Baptist Church, Daytona Beach, Florida; Board member of the Daytona Beach/Volusia County Salvation Army; Vice President, Volusia County Florida First Step Juvenile Residential Facility for young males; Board member of Volusia County Florida Children and Family Services; Committee member, Orlando, Orange County Florida, Juvenile Delinquency, Truancy, Crime and Behavioral Issues in Schools; and Committee member, Orlando, Orange County Florida, Juvenile Commission for Mental Health and Substance Abuse in Schools; Chair of the Board, Daytona Beach Housing Authority; Co-Chair, Daytona Beach, FL Charter Review Commission; Board member, Daytona Beach Personal Committee; Board member, Mid-Florida Head Start Policy Council.

**Dr. Kimmons** was selected in 2001 as a Distinguished Alumnus of his Alma Mater, Lincoln University, a Historical Black Institution located in Jefferson City, Missouri. He was recognized for his leadership skills, community involvement, scholarly pursuits, and educational achievements as an author, college professor, motivational speaker, college president and chancellor. In addition, the Distinguished Graduate award was bestowed upon Dr. Kimmons for exemplary service and for his contributions as an outstanding alumnus. The National Association for Equal Opportunity in Higher Education (NAFEO), also honored Dr. Kimmons at its 26th National Conference on Blacks in Higher Education held in Washington, D. C. in March, 2001.

**Dr. Kimmons** was the 2003 recipient of the <u>Furthering Rights, Investing in Equality and Nurturing Diversity</u> (F.R.I.E.N.D.) Award in Orlando

Florida. The Florida Civil Rights and Human Relations Commission honored him for his outstanding mentoring and volunteer work in public schools and the community.

**Dr. Kimmons** was the 2006 recipient of the National Alliance of Black School Educators, (NABSE), and Lifetime Achievement Award. NABSE honored him for his outstanding lifetime efforts and achievements to the African American community and the community at-large. This award was bestowed upon Dr. Kimmons at NABSE's Annual National Conference in Orlando, Florida.

**Dr. Kimmons** was inducted in the Frederick Douglass High School 2008 Wall of Fame for his scholarly pursuits, leadership skills, educational attainments in public schools, 2 and 4-year colleges and universities and as an honored graduate in Memphis, Tennessee.

**Dr. Kimmons** was honored as an outstanding community leader by the Daytona Deliverance Church of God in Daytona Beach, Florida, August, 2010. He was honored for his lifetime commitment of working with young people in the Volusia County Florida school system as a mentor and volunteer and his leadership in community activities, serving on numerous boards and advisory councils. He was commended for his service as a humanitarian, health care advocate and community activist which enriched the city, county and state in which he resides.

Dr. Willie Kimmons was recognized in 2012 by the National Alumni Association of Frederick Douglass High School for his continuous outstanding commitment and dedication to Frederick Douglass High School in Memphis, TN.

In 2013, Dr. Kimmons served as honored guest speaker on the Central Florida Good Life Television Program, channel 45, viewed by more than 5 million viewers in Orlando, FL.

Dr. Kimmons was honored as the Father of the Year at the 16th Annual International Fatherhood Conference and served as keynote speaker in June 2014 in Memphis, TN.

Dr. Kimmons was honored in 2016 as a former president of Trenholm State Community College in Montgomery, Alabama at the 50th Anniversary Celebration of the College. (1966-2016) for his professional commitment and dedication in stabilizing the College under his leadership as President.

2017, Dr. published his 5th book, "The Making of an Urban Community College in a Union and Political Environment: A Historical Perspective of Wayne County Community College District, Detroit, Michigan (1964-2017), where he served as President (1979-1983) of the Downtown Campus of Wayne County Community College.

2018, Dr. Kimmons was the recipient of the National Civil Rights and Social Justice Award for his lifelong commitment and his body of work in support of human dignity, civil rights and social justice. The award was presented during the 54th Anniversary Commemorative Service for James Chaney, Andrew Goodman and Michael Schwerner, the three young freedom fighters who were lynched in 1964 in Philadelphia, Mississippi. Dr. Kimmons also served as the keynote speaker at the awards ceremony.

2020, Dr. Kimmons served on the Daytona Beach, Florida branch of the NAACP, Board and Executive Committee.

2021 Dr. Kimmons published his 6th book, Parenting Forever Workbook for parents, grandparents and/or significant adults in the household to help save our children, save our schools. It is a youth diversion alternative program to give males and females, 17 and under, a second chance to sentencing, jail time and a permanent record. If the adult successfully completes the required training from the Parenting Forever Workbook's 7 modules, 3 Saturdays, 8 am-5 pm, the State Attorney and Judge may give the child a second chance to sentencing.

2022 Dr. Kimmons was the recipient of the Distinguished Alumnus Award by the Alumni Association of Northern Illinois University in DeKalb, Illinois. The award was given him because of his outstanding professional and personal success, achievements and national prominence in the field of education, his involvement in civic, community, cultural and charitable activities and as the author of 7 books. Dr. Kimmons received his Master's degree in Curriculum and Instruction (1970) and his doctorate in Education Administration and Supervision in Higher Education (1974) from Northern Illinois University.

2022 Dr. Kimmons published his 7$^{th}$ book, <u>The Personal, Private, Professional, Political Life and Legacy of the Honorable Shirley Anita St. Hill Chisholm-Hardwick</u>, his adopted godmother.

**Dr. Kimmons** has been awarded the key to 12 major cities in the United States by the mayors. He was honored and recognized for his community service, civic and leadership contributions in the areas of race relations and community relations.

**Dr. Willie J. Kimmons** is a religious man, family man, parent of four (4) adult children, two (2) daughters and two (2) sons, all of whom are graduates of Historically and Predominately Black Colleges and Universities (H.B.C.U.'s). Dr. Kimmons dedicated his current book, <u>A Parenting Guidebook</u>, to his seven (7) grandchildren, five (5) girls and two (2) boys.

In the past 5 years, Dr. Kimmons has spoken in 50 cities, signed and sold over 400,000 copies of his Parenting Guidebook. His godmother, the late, great, Honorable Shirley Chisholm, encouraged him to write <u>A Parenting Guidebook</u>. She wrote the foreword to his parenting guidebook.

**Dr. Kimmons'** interest in education stems from a background of training and experience in the area of human development, leadership, and community service. He is always eager to promote learning and development of the student by setting the atmosphere to motivate not only the student, but also other individuals within the educational arena.

**Dr. Willie J. Kimmons** has spent his entire career getting to the root of understanding the nature of the issues confronting today's parents, teachers, and students. He has successfully dealt with many of the challenges of human beings throughout his career as a professional educator and community activist. His life's ambition is to expand enthusiasm for education, and continue his commitment and dedication to the learner.

**Dr. Kimmons'** philosophy is … that institutions should be committed to providing quality educational and health care services and should be held accountable by the communities they serve. He welcomes the challenge of giving and sharing leadership that supports these goals. He further believes that by uniting our energies and supporting our educational and health care systems, we will be able to keep our students academically challenged, and our citizens better prepared for life.

**Dr. Kimmons'** Motto is …"Help Me to Help Somebody to Save Our Children, and Save Our Schools; Never, Ever, Give Up On Our Children, Because Our Children are Our Greatest Resource; Our Children are an Extension of Us; and Our Children are Our Future."

**Dr. Kimmons** is a new voice for partners in education. In 2005, he founded his corporation, Save Children Save Schools, Inc. Educational Services.

**Contact: Dr. Willie J. Kimmons**

**1653 Lawrence Circle**

**Daytona Beach, FL 32117**
**Office: 386-253-4920     Cell: 386-451-4780**

**E-mail: WJKimmons@aol.com**
**Website: www.savechildrensaveschools.com**

# CHAPTER 1

# INTRODUCTION

# THE EARLY YEARS: MAKING OF SHIRLEY ANITA ST. HILL CHISHOLM, GRANDMOTHER EMALINE SEALE, POLITICAL MENTOR, WESLEY MCDONALD HOLDER (MAX), OTHER COMMUNITY AND POLITICAL ACCOMPLISHMENTS

A narrative of the life and legacy of Shirley Anita St. Hill, later known as Shirley Chisholm. This is a modified version of a remarkable woman who made a significant difference in the lives of many, especially Black and brown women in the United States of America and the world. Mrs. Chisholm was multifaceted, multi-talented and fluent in speaking English and Spanish. She went from being born in Brooklyn, New York on November 30, 1924 in the Bedford-Stuyvesant community to visiting her grandmother and grandfather on the island of Barbados. Her grandmother had a thriving and highly productive farm called "The Seale's Farm", named after her grandparents. This is where little Shirley developed her knowledge of being self-sufficient and independent. Her grandparent's farm in Barbados was self-sustaining with the raising of many different farm animals and an assortment of different vegetable crops. Little Shirley began working on the farm and developing the work ethics of her grandparents early in life. She spent many hours with her grandmother Seale. Grandmother Seale recognized that little Shirley had special talents, was a quick learner and extremely obedient. Shirley began school and mastered most of her classes quickly. Her grandmother Seale began to spoil little Shirley early on by instilling in her about life and always reminded her that she was beautiful, smart and always to believe in herself. Her grandmother told her that she was "special". "God gave you many unusual traits in life to use and share with others as you grow up." Mrs. Shirley Chisholm credits her grandmother, Emaline Seale, who raised her when she lived in Barbados from age 3 to 9, as a source of strength, dignity and love. She also credits her mother, Ruby Seale, for inspiring her as a model for moral authority and conviction.

Little Shirley was taught by her grandmother the importance of reading, writing, speaking, having pride, dignity and class as a Black Female. As a result of all these attributes, little Shirley read everything, magazines, the bible, and all kinds of books and newspapers in many different languages.

Little Shirley Anita St. Hill was reading at 3 (the Bible), and recalls that visitors would "always pick me out as the bright one in the family." This was a frequent enough occurrence for early hostility to develop between Shirley and her three sisters. The rift that became permanent when, in his will, Shirley's father left her a small inheritance, to the exclusion of the rest of the family. "Even as a child," she admits, "I couldn't understand why most people couldn't think like I do."

She credits her father, Charles Christopher St. Hill, a devoted follower of a visionary, civil rights leader of Black people, Marcus Garvey, for igniting her political consciousness and supporting her leadership aspirations. Shirley Chisholm had a close relationship with her father. He truly adored and admired her intellect, drive and her fighting ability for human rights and civil rights. Shirley Chisholm was her daddy's pride and joy, the apple of his eye. However, she didn't realize that this created a serious rift between her mother and her 3 sisters. The jealously was extremely painful and vicious to her. The family relationship never recovered.

She grew up and returned to Brooklyn, New York around the age of 9 and later attended the prestigious Girls High School. Her extraordinary talents were immediately recognized by everyone including her teachers and fellow students. She was elected by the student body as Vice President to a club of academically gifted students.

She became a community organizer, working with local groups discussing and addressing the problems of poor people, women's groups, children and Black and brown people. Shirley realized as a nursery school teacher, because of her love for children, that there were many pressing needs of the people she was teaching and serving. After her first marriage to Conrad Chisholm in 1949, she realized her second passion was politics, community involvement and being a public servant. This is when she started seriously planning her political career.

She started working with neighborhood communities, religious and women's groups. This is when she met her political guru, Mr. Max Holder, a Black man known for his political and community savvy. He mentored and developed numerous Black and brown politicians who successfully became elected officials. Mr. Max Holder helped Mrs. Chisholm in Brooklyn, New York to orchestrate her first successful political campaign. He saw in her a natural born community and political leader with a tremendous amount of skill and smarts with a fighting attitude. This propelled her political career and name recognition in Brooklyn and throughout the city of New York.

Shirley Chisholm remembered the teaching of her grandmother Seale in Barbados to always believe in herself and that she could be and do anything in life that she wanted as long as she properly prepared herself. Grandmother Seale instilled in Shirley her 5 P's of life: prior planning prevents poor performance. That has been Shirley Chisholm's road map to success in politics and life.

She was a New York Assembly woman from 1964 to 1968. Mrs. Chisholm was elected to the U. S. Congress in 1968 and ran for the Presidency of the United States in 1972. As a result of these accomplishments, Shirley became known as "Fighting Shirley Chisholm", "A Catalyst for Change", "Unbought and Unbossed" and "The Good Fight".

God bless my adopted godmother for mentoring and assisting me in life to be the Black man I am today. One may never know how many children, women, adults, young and old, white, Black and brown people Mrs. Chisolm may have inspired, motivated, encouraged, educated, enlightened to be all they can be. But you can see all the positive results in the political organizations she helped to create for women and people of color. You can see the results in the Black elected women and men that are in political offices at every level, local, state, regional, district and national.

I am a living witness of Mrs. Shirley Chisholm's influence and impact on my life personally and professionally. As the oldest of 27 children, 16 sisters and 11 brothers, born in Hernando, Mississippi. I chopped and picked cotton for $3.00 a day and attended a one-room schoolhouse in

3

rural Mississippi. After serving in the United States Army as an officer, I received a doctorate degree at the age of 28. Then I became a public-school teacher, college professor, dean, vice president, president, chancellor, motivational speaker, author of six books, community leader and public servant.

Mrs. Chisholm inspired me to write my 5th book, <u>A Parenting Guidebook</u> for parents, grandparents, teachers, schools, communities and churches to help save our children and save our schools. She wrote the foreword to my book<u>, A Parenting Guidebook</u> in Ormond Beach, Florida before her untimely death on January 1, 2005.

Shirley Chisholm was the oldest with three sisters, Odesa, Muriel and Selma, born to immigrant parents. Her father was Charles Christopher St. Hill, a factory worker from Guyana and her mother was Ruby Seale St. Hill, a seamstress from Barbados. Shirley graduated from Brooklyn Girls High in 1942, earned a bachelor of science degree from Brooklyn College in 1946, Cum Laude, and a Master's degree in Elementary Education from Columbia university in 1952. She spent part of her early childhood years with her grandmother in Barbados where she acquired her accent and Spanish speaking skills.

Her political mentor/advisor was Max Holder, who also served as a political advisor to many Black politicians in the New York area for years. He was referred to as the "Dean of Black politics". Mr. Holder helped propel Shirley Chisholm's career. She represented Brooklyn, New York's 12th Congressional District for seven terms from 1969 to 1983. Her legacy of political and social activism laid the foundation for the rise of women and Blacks in American politics.

In 1971, Congresswoman Chisholm became the first woman and founding member of both the Congressional Black Caucus and the National Women's Political Caucus. In 1964, she became the second black woman elected to the New York State Assembly and 4 years later, 1968, because of redistricting, a seat became open in the National House of Representatives for her district of Bedford-Stuyvesant in Brooklyn, New York. She ran for Congress in 1968 against the powerful Black activist, James Farmer, founder of CORE, (Congress of Racial Equality). Mr. Farmer did not take Mrs. Chisholm's candidacy seriously. He saw her as a tiny non-threatening Black lady, and nothing he and his supporters had to worry about. But Mr. Farmer grossly underestimated this little, Black, but powerful, political, educated lady. During their debates for the 1968 Congressional seat, Mr. Farmer didn't realize that many of the constituents in the Bedford-Stuyvesant Congressional District were from the Caribbean Islands and spoke fluent Spanish and English, just like Mrs. Chisholm. Many of the debates were done in Spanish and since Mr. Farmer did not speak Spanish fluently, he seemed to have been thoroughly frustrated.

As a result of this, Mrs. Chisholm garnered more than 67% of all the registered voters. James Farmer never recovered. It was the shock of his life. Later, when Mr. Farmer died from diabetes complications, Shirley Chisholm was kind enough to attend and participate in his funeral.

Shirley Chisholm worked in education as a teacher and social services, counseling and advising people in New York before being elected to the New York State Assembly in 1964. She established the Unity Democratic Club in 1960, which played a significant role in rallying Black and Hispanic voters. She inspired and led the march of political achievements for African Americans, especially Black and Brown women, prior to seeking the Presidency of the United States. Her election to Congress in 1968 and her candidacy for the Presidency in 1972 raised the profile and aspirations of all African Americans and women in the field of politics. In 2014, the U. S. Postal Service issued the 37th Black Heritage Forever Stamp, with an image of Shirley Chisholm. She inspired President Barak Obama in 2008, Hillary Clinton in 2016 and Vice President Kamala Harris in 2020 to seek the highest political office. Congresswoman Shirley Chisholm was recognized for her activism, independence and ground breaking achievements in politics during and after the Civil Rights Era.

During her 14 years of service in the House of Representatives, Congresswoman Chisholm promoted the employment of women in Congress. She was extremely vocal in her support of civil rights, women's rights and the poor, while fervently opposing the Vietnam War.

In 1984 she co-founded with C. Delores Tucker, The National Congress of Black Women which was to encourage, promote and recruit Black and brown women to get involved in the political process. Also, to run for office at the local, regional, district and national levels. Hundreds of Black women benefited from the establishment of that organization. Women, Black, white and brown who seek political office are indebted to

Shirley Chisholm for her insight, vision and leadership as a role model and Catalyst for change. As a result of her bold move as a risk-taker and change agent in the dominate male, particularly white male political arena, she paved the way for many women. Mrs. Chisholm was a trend setter. She defied the odds against white men, Black men, white women and Black women. She stood alone and still succeeded.

Shirley Chisholm was a teacher, scholar, orator, intellectual and public servant. Her lifelong work continues to shape the American social and political landscape today. Chisholm's two outstanding books, Unbought and Unbossed in 1970 and The Good Fight in 1973, speaks volumes of struggles in her personal and political life.

In 1990 Congresswoman Chisholm co-founded the African American Women for Reproductive Freedom. She was inducted in the National Women's Hall of Fame in 1993. As a result of her outstanding achievements, she received a posthumous Presidential Medal of Freedom from President Barack Obama in 2015. Congresswoman Shirley Chisholm was also posthumously awarded the Congressional Gold Medal by Congress in 2018.

According to the Congressional Black Caucus records, they have done a thorough account of African American women in Congress. In 1969, Shirley A. Chisholm became the first African American woman to serve in Congress after being elected to represent New York's 12th district in the U.S. House of Representatives. Representative Chisholm was also a founding member and the only female of the Congressional Black Caucus in 1971.

As of 2020 there are about 120 women in the U.S. House of Representatives; 25 women in the U.S. Senate; 5 women have served on the Supreme Court and 43 women have served as state governors with 1 woman as Vice President of the United States. There have been hundreds of women elected to political offices at the local and state levels. These Black, brown and white women benefitted from Mrs. Chisholm's election as a Congresswoman since 1968. Thank God for the Honorable Shirley Chisholm's contribution for all the outstanding women who have served in various political positions across this country. They have made a tremendous impact on raising the awareness of gender bias, social injustice and racial issues. The Congressional Black Caucus noted that there have been 50 African American women elected to Congress from 1968 to 2020.

*Mrs. Chisholm*

# CHAPTER 2

## THE IMPACT CONGRESSWOMAN CHISHOLM HAD ON MY LIFE AND THE INFLUENCE OF ABOLITIONIST FREDERICK DOUGLASS AND AUTHOR DR. CARTER G. WOODSON HAD ON HER AND ME

Knowledge is power and no one can take it away from you. This is the reason we need to showcase the political contributions of Congresswoman Chisholm. Our young people and people of all ages and races should know the name Shirley Chisholm and what she stood for.

As the adopted godson of the late, great, Honorable Shirley Chisholm, I was asked to write a brief narrative detailing the life and legacy of Mrs. Chisholm. This narrative will address her political accomplishments, her family life and her personal view points about her grandparents in Barbados, especially her relationship with her Grandmother Seale.

The narrative outlines Mrs. Chisholm's drive to achieving her career path as a teacher, educator, public servant, community leader and a strong, vocal African American female. She has been in my life for many years. Congresswoman Chisholm was present at every college/university where I worked as a college dean, vice president, president and chancellor. Many years ago in 1977, I served as an academic Dean at St. Francis College in Brooklyn, New York which was near her 12th Congressional District. Later on, I served as Dean of the College of Education at the University of the District of Columbia (UDC) when she was a member of the U.S. Congress in Washington, D.C.

Mrs. Chisholm has been an inspiration to me and my educational, spiritual, and developmental success. She has served as a positive role model for me and thousands of people in this country and the world. So, this is why I am interested in giving her the proper respect and honor she so rightfully deserves. My role as her assigned godson is to properly orientate and

8

educate people, especially Black and brown women about her outstanding accomplishments. Hundreds of Black, brown and white women in the political arena are standing on the shoulders of the Honorable Shirley Chisholm. The women who sought the office of Congress, President and Vice-President from the nineteen seventies through 2020, all are indebted to Mrs. Chisholm for her insights, courage, vision and leadership role. Her landmark and favorite statement is that she is "a catalyst for change".

As a result of her bold move as a risk-taker and change agent in this male, particularly dominated white and male political arena, she paved the way for women, especially Black and brown females. Congresswoman Chisholm was a trend setter, defying the odds against white men, Black men, white women and some Black women in most cases. After all these distractions, she stood alone and still succeeded politically.

When I think of the Honorable Shirley Chisholm, I'm often reminded of her tremendous commitment to humanity, mankind and her people. She has always been a student of Frederick Douglass and Dr. Carter G. Woodson. Once a year Mrs. Chisholm would read their most enlightening quotations. She quoted the Honorable Frederick Douglass, writer, orator, abolitionist, freedom fighter, spokesperson and civil rights leader. Dr. Carter G. Woodson, an outstanding educator, founder of Black History Month and world renown author of his most famous book, "The Mis-education of the Negro", (1933) was also quoted.

When I think of the crisis of today in the Black and brown communities, I am often reminded of the sayings of the abolitionist Frederick Douglass: "If there is no struggle, there is no progress. Those who profess to favor freedom, and yet deprecate agitation, are men who want rain without thunder and lightning. They want the ocean without the awful roar of its many waters. This struggle may be a moral one; or it may be a physical one; or it may be moral and physical, but it must be a struggle. Power concedes nothing without a demand. It never did and never will." Also, I'm citing the comments of African American historian, educator and founder of Black History Month, Dr. Carter G. Woodson. "When you control a man's thinking, you do not have to worry about his actions. You do not have to tell him not to stand here or go yonder. He will find his proper place and will stay in it. You do not need to send him to the back door, he will go without being told. In fact, if there is no back door, he will cut one for his special benefit. In a crisis in the Black and *brown communities, history shows that it does not matter who is in power; those who have not learned to do for themselves and have to depend solely on others never obtain any more rights or privileges in the end than they had in the beginning.*" We are indebted to these two courageous African American men which is why we are pleased to produce and publish this narrative about their impact on Shirley Chisholm's life and legacy.

Mrs. Chisholm would spend hours reading the great works of abolitionist Frederick Douglass and Dr. Carter G. Woodson to me in her homes in Palm Coast and Ormond Beach, Florida where she died January 1, 2005 at the tender age of 80.

I am going to list some excerpts from Frederick Douglass' 4th of July speech, "What to the Slave is the 4th of July", and Carter G. Woodson's book, <u>The Mis-Education of the Negro.</u>

As one who is a life-long student of the Honorable Frederick Douglass, I decided to share my thoughts about the 4th of July celebration. So many of us are spending a considerable amount of time showing our appreciation for the 4th of July by celebrating this so-called "freedom" and joyous event. I'm listing a historical perspective for my Black, brown and white brothers and sisters.

First, we need to clearly understand what this 4th of July celebration means to African Americans. Secondly, we need to study and analyze our history as opposed to being studied and analyzed by others. As African Americans, this should be a day to research, read, discuss and share the true meaning of this day with our children's, children's children for years to come.

As a race of people, let us learn to appreciate and acknowledge our ancestor's struggle for freedom. We should know and understand what our forefathers endured to survive the cruel and inhumane treatment. While others celebrate the 4th of July, our slave ancestors, were building this country on their backs as free laborers. As of today, they remain unpaid for their labor. Are we really "free"? Are we, as African Americans and people of color in a position to really celebrate? It has been over 169 years since the Honorable Frederick Douglass, orator and abolitionist, gave his most famous speech on July 5th 1852 in Rochester, New York entitled, "What to the slave is the 4th of July?" This, my brothers and sisters, is the question we need to address as we witness, daily, the constant assault on our civil liberties, democratic values and civil rights as African Americans and people of color in this country.

I will share an abbreviated and paraphrased version of Frederick Douglass' July 5,1852 speech and an excerpt of his famous saying. Hopefully, we can find some time during the 4th of July celebration to read and share these extremely important words as Frederick Douglass so eloquently elaborated on in "What to the slave is the 4th of July?".

Unfortunately, my brothers and sisters, we as African Americans, are experiencing and living these same misdeeds today in this country. This means very little, if any, progress has been made when it comes to race relations and social justice for our people.

Mrs. Chisholm spent most of her career reading the great works of Frederick Douglass and Carter G. Woodson. She was inspired by their wit, knowledge base, writing and speaking skills. The two bodies of works that commanded a great deal of her time were: Frederick Douglass' Fourth of July, 1852 Speech in Rochester, New York, in which he refused to deliver on the 4th of July. He gave the famous speech on the 5th of July, mainly because of his opposition against whites celebrating the 4th of July as a day to acknowledge all the great things the United States had accomplished and how well the country had treated its citizens. Mrs. Chisholm personally noted one portion of Frederick Douglass' 5th of July Speech which she compares this part to African Americans' plight today and what the 4th of July really means to Black people. The response from Frederick Douglass says: *"What to the American slave, is your 4th of July? I answer: A Day that reveals to him, more than all other days in the year, the gross injustice and cruelty to which he is the constant victim. To him, your celebration is a sham; your boasted liberty, an unholy license; your national greatness, swelling vanity; your sounds of rejoicing are empty and heartless; your denunciation of tyrants, brass fronted impudence; Your shouts of liberty and equality, hollow mockery; your prayers and hymns, your sermons and thanksgiving with all your religious parade, and solemnity are to him, mere bombast, fraud, deception, impiety, and hypocrisy in a thin veil to cover up crimes which would disgrace a nation of savages. There is not a nation on the earth guilty of practices more shocking and bloodier, than are the people of these United States at this very hour".*

*Frederick Douglass 1818-1895*

This is an abridged version by Janet Gillespie of the Honorable Frederick Douglass' Fourth of July 5, 1852 speech. This is what Congresswoman Chisholm would read to me and we would discuss every Fourth of July until her untimely death, January 1, 2005.

*"He who could address this audience without a quailing sensation, has stronger nerves than I have. I do not remember ever to have appeared as a speaker before any assembly more shrinkingly, nor with greater distrust of my ability, than I do this day. A feeling has crept over me quite unfavorable to the exercise of my limited powers of speech. The task before me is one which requires much previous thought and study for its proper performance. I know that apologies of this sort are generally considered flat and unmeaning. I trust, however, that mine will not be so considered. Should I seem at ease, my appearance would much misrepresent me. The little experience I have had in addressing public meetings, in country school houses, avails me nothing on the present occasion.*

*The fact is, ladies and gentlemen, the distance between this platform and the slave plantation, from which I escaped, is considerable-and the difficulties to be overcome in getting from the latter to the former are by no means slight. That I am here to-day is, to me, a matter of astonishment as well as of gratitude. You will not, therefore, be surprised, if in what I have to say I evince no elaborate preparation, nor grace my speech with any high sounding exordium. With little experience and with less learning, I have been able to throw my thoughts hastily and imperfectly together; and trusting to your*

12

*patient and generous indulgence I will proceed to lay them before you. This, for the purpose of this celebration, is the Fourth of July. It is the birth day of your National Independence, and of your political freedom. This, to you, is what the Passover was to the emancipated people of God. It carries your minds back to the day, and to the act of your great deliverance; and to the signs, and to the wonders, associated with that act, and that day. This celebration also marks the beginning of another year of your national life; and reminds you that the Republic of America is now 76 years old. l am glad, fellow-citizens, that your nation is so young. Seventy-six years, though a good old age for a man, is but a mere speck in the life of a nation. Three score years and ten is the allotted time for individual men; but nations number their years by thousands.*

*Friends and citizens, I need not enter further into the causes which led to this anniversary. Many of you understand them better than I do. You could instruct me in regard to them. That is a branch of knowledge in which you feel, perhaps, a much deeper interest than your speaker. The causes which led to the separation of the colonies from the British crown have never lacked for a tongue. They have all been taught in your common schools, narrated at your firesides, unfolded from your pulpits, and thundered from your legislative halls, and are as familiar to you as household words. They form the staple of your national poetry and eloquence.*

*I remember, also, that, as a people, Americans are remarkably familiar with all facts which are made in their own favor. This is esteemed by some as a national trait-perhaps a national weakness. It is a fact, that whatever makes for the wealth or for the reputation of Americans and can be had cheap will be found by Americans. I shall not be charged with slandering Americans if I say I think the American side of any question may be safely left in American hands.*

*I leave, therefore, the great deeds of your fathers to other gentlemen whose claim to have been regularly descended will be less likely to be disputed than mine!*

*My business, if I have any here to-day, is with the present. The accepted time with God and His cause is the ever-living now.*

> *Trust no future, however pleasant,*
> *Let the dead past bury its dead;*
> *Act, act in the living present,*
> *Heart within, and God overhead.*

*Fellow-citizens, pardon me, allow me to ask, why am I called upon to speak here to-day? What have I, or those I represent, to do with your national independence? Are the great principles of political freedom and of natural justice, embodied in that Declaration of Independence, extended to us? and am I, therefore, called upon to bring our humble offering to the national altar, and to confess the benefits and express devout gratitude for the blessings resulting from your independence to us?*

*Fellow-citizens, above your national, tumultuous joy, I hear the mournful wail of millions! whose chains, heavy and grievous yesterday, are, to-day, rendered more intolerable by the jubilee shouts that reach them. If I do forget, if I do not faithfully remember those bleeding children of sorrow this day, "may my right hand forget her cunning, and may my tongue cleave to the roof of my mouth!" To forget them, to pass lightly over their wrongs, and to chime in with the popular theme, would be treason most scandalous and shocking, and would make me a reproach before God and the world. My subject, then, fellow-citizens, is AMERICAN SLAVERY. I shall see this day and its popular characteristics from the slave's point of view. Standing there identified with the American bondman, making his wrongs mine, I do not hesitate to declare, with all my soul, that the character and conduct of this nation never looked blacker to me than on this 4th of July! Whether we turn to the declarations of the past, or to the professions of the present, the conduct of the nation seems equally hideous and revolting. America is false to the past, false to the present, and solemnly binds herself to be false to the future. Standing with God and the crushed and bleeding slave on this occasion, I will, in the name of humanity which is outraged, in the name of liberty which is fettered, in the name of the constitution and the Bible which are disregarded and trampled upon, dare to call in question and to denounce, with all the emphasis I can command, everything that serves to perpetuate slavery-the great sin and shame of America! "I will not equivocate; I will not excuse"; I will use the severest language I can command; and yet not one word shall escape me that any man, whose judgment is not blinded by prejudice, or who is not at heart a slaveholder, shall not confess to be right and just. But I fancy I hear some one of my audience say, "It is just in this circumstance that you and your brother abolitionists fail to make a favorable impression on the public mind. Would you argue more, and denounce less; would you persuade more, and rebuke less; your cause would be much more likely to succeed." But, I submit, where all is plain there is nothing to be argued. What point in the anti-slavery creed would you have me argue? On what branch of the subject do the people of this country need light? Must I undertake to prove that the slave is a man? That point is conceded already. Nobody doubts it. The slaveholders themselves acknowledge it in the enactment of laws for their government. They acknowledge it when they punish disobedience on the part of the slave. There are seventy-two crimes in the State of Virginia which, if committed by a black man (no matter how ignorant he be), subject him to the punishment of death; while only two of the same crimes will subject a white man to the like punishment. What is this but the acknowledgment that the slave is a moral, intellectual, and responsible being?*

*For the present, it is enough to affirm the equal manhood of the Negro race. Is it not astonishing that, while we are ploughing, planting, and reaping, using all kinds of mechanical tools, erecting houses, constructing bridges, building ships, working in metals of brass, iron, copper, silver and gold; that, while we are reading, writing and ciphering, acting as clerks, merchants and secretaries, having among us lawyers, doctors, ministers, poets, authors, editors, orators and teachers; that, while we are engaged in all manner of enterprises common to other men, digging gold in California, capturing the whale in the Pacific, feeding sheep and cattle on the hill-side, living, moving, acting, thinking, planning, living in families as husbands, wives and children, and, above all, confessing and worshipping the Christian's God, and looking hopefully for life and immortality beyond the grave, we are called upon to prove that we are men!*

*Would you have me argue that man is entitled to liberty? that he is the rightful owner of his own body? You have already declared it. Must I argue the wrongfulness of slavery? Is that a question for Republicans? Is it to be settled by the rules of logic and argumentation, as a matter beset with great difficulty, involving a doubtful application of the principle of justice, hard to be understood? How should I look to-day, in the presence of Americans, dividing, and subdividing a discourse, to show that men have a natural right to freedom speaking of it relatively and positively, negatively and affirmatively. To do so, would be to make myself ridiculous, and to offer an insult to your understanding. --There is not a man beneath the canopy of heaven that does not know that slavery is wrong for him.*

*The American church is guilty, when viewed in connection with what it is doing to uphold slavery; but it is superlatively guilty when viewed in its connection with its ability to abolish slavery. The sin of which it is guilty is one of omission as well as of commission. Albert Barnes uttered what the common sense of every man at all observant of the actual state of the case will receive as truth, when he declared that "There is no power out of the church that could sustain slavery an hour, if it were not sustained in it."*

*Let the religious press, the pulpit, the Sunday School, the conference meeting, the great ecclesiastical, missionary, Bible and tract associations of the land array their immense powers against slavery, and slave-holding; and the whole system of crime and blood would be scattered to the winds, and that they do not do this involves them in the most awful responsibility of which the mind can conceive.*

*Allow me to say, in conclusion, notwithstanding the dark picture I have this day presented, of the state of the nation, I do not despair of this country. There are forces in operation which must inevitably work the downfall of slavery. "The arm of the Lord is not shortened," and the doom of slavery is certain. I, therefore, leave off where I began, with hope.*

*While drawing encouragement from "the Declaration of Independence," the great principles it contains, and the genius of American Institutions, my spirit is also cheered by the obvious tendencies of the age. Nations do not now stand in the same relation to each other that they did ages ago. No nation can now shut itself up from the surrounding world and trot round in the same old path of its fathers without interference. The time was when such could be done. Long established customs of hurtful character could formerly fence themselves in, and do their evil work with social impunity. Knowledge was then confined and enjoyed by the privileged few, and the multitude walked on in mental darkness. But a change has now come over the affairs of mankind. Walled cities and empires have become unfashionable. The arm of commerce has borne away the gates of the strong city. Intelligence is penetrating the darkest corners of the globe. It makes its pathway over and under the sea, as well as on the earth. Wind, steam, and lightning are its chartered agents. Oceans no longer divide, but link nations together. From Boston to London is now a holiday excursion. Space is comparatively annihilated. Thoughts expressed on one side of the Atlantic are distinctly heard on the other. The far off and almost fabulous Pacific rolls in grandeur at our feet. The Celestial Empire, the mystery of ages, is being solved. The fiat of the Almighty, "Let there be Light," has not yet spent its force. No abuse, no outrage whether in taste, sport or avarice, can now hide itself from the all-pervading light. The iron shoe, and crippled foot of China must be seen in contrast with nature. Africa must rise and put on her yet unwoven garment. "Ethiopia shall stretch out her hand unto God." In the fervent aspirations of William Lloyd Garrison, I say, and let every heart join in saying it:*

> *God speed the year of jubilee*
> *The wide world o'er!*
> *When from their galling chains set free,*
> *Th' oppress'd shall vilely bend the knee,*
> *And wear the yoke of tyranny*
> *Like brutes no more.*
> *That year will come, and freedom's reign.*
> *To man his plundered rights again*
> *Restore.*
> *God speed the day when human blood*
> *Shall cease to flow!*
> *In every clime be understood,*
> *The claims of human brotherhood,*
> *And each return for evil, good,*
> *Not blow for blow;*
> *That day will come all feuds to end,*
> *And change into a faithful friend*
> *Each foe.*
> *God speed the hour, the glorious hour,*
> *When none on earth*
> *Shall exercise a lordly power,*
> *Nor in a tyrant's presence cower;*
> *But all to manhood's stature tower,*
> *By equal birth!*
> *That hour will come, to each, to all,*
> *And from his prison-house, the thrall*
> *Go forth.*

*Until that year, day, hour, arrive,*
*With head, and heart, and hand I'll strive,*
*To break the rod, and rend the gyve,*
*The spoiler of his prey deprive - So witness Heaven!*
*And never from my chosen post,*
*Whate'er the peril or the cost.*
*Be driven."*

After reading the great words of Frederick Douglass and excerpts from his famous speech, "What to the slaves is the 4th of July?" I'm reminded of a response I shared with my high school classmates in Memphis, Tennessee at Frederick Douglass High School. History provides abundant examples of people whose greatest gift was in redeeming, inspiring, liberating, and nurturing the gifts of others. Therefore, embrace our past and learn our history.

I am a 1962 distinguished and proud graduate of Frederick Douglass High School. I have been a life-long student and researcher of the Honorable Frederick Douglass for more than 40 years. I reminded my classmates that at the time of Frederick Douglass' speech, July 5,1852 and the Declaration of Independence,1776, Black folks, were slaves and had <u>no rights.</u> Today,170 years and 246 years later respectively, (2022), we are still enslaved and not free. In the past, white folks, through fear and intimidation, didn't want Black folks relating to an abolitionist like Frederick Douglass. The age-old tactics they used, historically, had us physically hanging from trees. Today, they have control over many of us mentally and physically. When a man has your mind and body, he has complete control over you. As Black people in Memphis, we are still saying Douglass Schools, Douglass churches and Douglass Community, not <u>Frederick </u>Douglass Schools, <u>Frederick</u> Douglass churches and the <u>Frederick</u> Douglass Community.

As stated in the National Museum of African American History and Culture in 2016, African Americans changed the course of the Civil War by engaging President Lincoln in ongoing debates. Frederick Douglass used his renowned oratory and his power as an abolitionist leader to <u>demand</u> that President Lincoln take action. First, to use his position as President to end slavery; second, if he wanted to enlist African Americans to fight in a liberating army, then grant full citizenship to all African Americans. However, based on the strategic need to increase military support to win the Civil War, through Frederick Douglass' influence, President Lincoln supported and included Black soldiers as a provision of the Emancipation Proclamation which ultimately freed the slaves in America.

I'm convinced that President Abraham Lincoln did not free the slaves. Lincoln was a politician who was more interested in winning the war between the North and South. He sought out Frederick Douglass for assistance to have Black men lay down their life for his political expediency. Winning the war was more important to Lincoln's presidency than the freedom of slaves in this country. So, the negotiation between abolitionist Frederick Douglass and President Abraham Lincoln became a reality. Douglass stated firmly and directly to Lincoln, "If you want my Black brothers to fight and die for you, then free my Black people." This, my friends, was the beginning of freedom from slavery in America. Thank God for the wisdom, foresight, courage, strength and vision the great Frederick Douglass had during these deliberations and negotiations for Black people to be free.

In 1860 after the election of President Abraham Lincoln, he did not begin his term with a goal to end slavery. His military goal was to keep the Union together. African Americans were determined to win their fight for freedom by any means necessary. With the powerful debates and strong encouraging conversations Frederick Douglass had with President Lincoln, on January 1, 1863, the Emancipation Proclamation went into effect declaring that <u>all persons enslaved were free.</u> It should be obvious to all readers, <u>who really freed the slaves</u>. After this interesting and fierce relationship, President Abraham Lincoln and abolitionist Frederick Douglass stood as the two most influential figures in the middle of the 19th Century.

Therefore, it is crucial, that we know, appreciate, respect and share our rich history and the valuable contributions Blacks have made in our community, city, state, country and the world. I repeat, we need to study and analyze ourselves as opposed to being studied and analyzed by others. Always, study, and do critical, accurate research about our people and share with our children's, children's, children's, children. If you don't know your history, especially from a true and positive perspective, you are doomed to fail and continue to repeat the negative, We, as a race of people, have a rich history and it needs to be shared, told and documented. This is what my adopted godmother, former Congresswoman Chisholm instilled in me, through the years, the rich history and contributions of the Honorable Frederick Douglass and Dr. Carter G. Woodson.

Some background information about Dr. Carter G. Woodson's great works that always interested Congresswoman Chisholm was his educational and intellectual skills. He was the second African American to receive a doctorate degree from Harvard University after W. E. B. DuBois.

*Dr. Carter G. Woodson, born 1875, Died 1950*

Carter G. Woodson stated: *"How an 'educated Negro' can thus leave the church of his people and accept such Jim Crowism has always been a puzzle. He cannot be a thinking man. It may be a sort of slave psychology which causes this preference for the leadership of the oppressor. The excuse sometimes given for seeking such religious leadership is that the Negro evangelical churches are "fogy," but a thinking man would rather be behind the times and have his self-respect than compromise his manhood by accepting segregation. They say that in some of the Negro churches bishoprics are actually bought, but it is better for the Negro to belong to a church where one can secure a bishopric by purchase than be a member of one which would deny the promotion on account of color."*

Dr. Carter G. Woodson was an African American historian and educator, the founder of Negro History Month and the founder of The Association for the Study of Negro Life and History. He was the author of more than 16 books; the founder and editor of The Journal of Negro History and The Negro History Bulletin. Dr. Woodson's most famous masterpiece book is <u>The Mis-education of the Negro</u>, (1933).

The creative works of these two historical, educational, civil rights and political giants has been a driving force in Mrs. Chisholm's political and civil rights life. Her father also admired Frederick Douglass and Carter G. Woodson's commitment to decency and human dignity. Unfortunately, we as African Americans are experiencing and living these same misdeeds today in this country. Which means very little, if any, progress has been made when it comes to race relations and social justice.

*My godmother, The Honorable Shirley Chisholm and me.*

# CHAPTER 3

# THE IMPACT FOUR POWERFUL WOMEN HAD ON SEXISM, RACISM, CIVIL RIGHTS AND POLITICS: FANNIE LOU HAMER, SHIRLEY CHISHOLM, HARRIET TUBMAN AND SOJOURNER TRUTH

*1797-1883*    *1820-1913*

*1917-1977*    *1924-2005*

The thoughts brought together in this narrative will be expressed throughout the document by the author. The wording in some cases in this narrative is entirely new and the great work is a collection of one-on-one conversations with Congresswoman Chisholm, her friends and adopted godson, Dr. Willie J. Greer Kimmons. In this way, a concerted effort has been made to avoid and eliminate repetition. I want to personally thank Wikipedia, the free encyclopedia for granting me permission to cite these comments of four great, Black women in American history.

When I think of the life and legacy of the Honorable Shirley Chisholm, I'm often reminded of these comments of four great Black women:

1. Fannie Lou Hamer.... Is known as the lady who made the famous expression *"I am sick and tired of being sick and tired,"* in regard to the struggle to gain civil rights in Mississippi. She was born, October 6, 1917 in Montgomery County, Ruleville, Mississippi. She died March 14, 1977 in Mound Bayou, Mississippi. She was beaten and jailed in Winona, Mississippi for attempting to register to vote. While she was traveling on a bus on June 3, 1963, state law enforcement officers in Winona, Mississippi took Hamer and fellow activists to Montgomery County jail where they were severely beaten.

   She testified that she was beaten until her *"body was hard."* She suffered a blood clot, severe damage to her kidneys, and required a month to recover from the assault. As an instrumental figure in the struggle for civil rights, Hamer co-founded the Mississippi Freedom Democratic Party (MFDP). In 1964, the MFDP challenged the all-white Mississippi delegation to the Democratic National Convention. Hamer spoke to the Credentials Committee members in a televised proceeding that reached millions of viewers. She told the committee how African Americans in many states across the country were prevented from voting through illegal tests, taxes, and intimidation tactics. As a result of her speech, two delegates of the MFDP were permitted to speak at the convention and the other members were seated as honorable guests (Women had key roles in the civil rights movement). Mrs. Hamer stated, *"One day I know the struggle will change. There's got to be a change, not only for Mississippi, not only for the people in the United States, but people all over the world."* Unfortunately, today we are still experiencing the same intimidating tactics with many road blocks denying and discouraging Black and brown people from voting.

2. In 1972, when Mrs. Chisholm was running for President of the United States, she had an encounter with Senators John Lindsay and George McGovern. John V. Lindsay invited Shirley Chisholm

to Gracie Mansion. Over a dram of Yuletide cheer, the Mayor of New York urged the Congresswoman from Bedford Stuyvesant to abandon her quixotic quest for the Presidency so that he could more successfully pursue his. But Fighting Shirley Chisholm, as she likes to call herself, wasn't having any of it. She remembers that the conversation went like this:

*"Shirley, are you're serious about running for the Presidency,"* Lindsay sighed?

*"How many times do I have to tell you?"* Mrs. Chisholm told him yet again.

*"But, Shirley, it takes thousands…"*

*"It takes millions, I know that…But I'm the only candidate who's black and a woman…You're my friend, but I'm so goddam fed up with all this s--- you men keep putting down. You've got the media. You've got the money. I go out and get maybe five, six people to a meeting, and the press reports is…But you got the money to go out and bring people in by the busloads so it looks like you get good crowds all the time…"*

"Shirley," Lindsay soothed, *"you'll cut into my vote."*

*"That's the same thing McGovern told me,"* Mrs. Chisholm snapped. *"But goddam it, this is the American Dream-the chance for a black woman to run for the highest office. If you're so worried about cutting into the progressive vote, why don't you and McGovern get together—and one of you decide to back out?"*

It was a delicious, if fleeting, moment for Shirley Anita St. Hill Chisholm and, through her, for Black Politics, 1972. On that day, those men whom George Wallace had termed "the face cards in the Democratic deck"—from glamorous, well-heeled, new-kid-on the-block John Lindsay, to the now-likely Democratic nominee, Senator George McGovern—were scared that Shirley Chisholm and black voters would gang up to blunt their drives for the Democratic nomination.

But it was not to be the lofty dream of black politicians— to overcome their own personal prejudices and ambitions, and coalesce into a powerful force in Presidential politics—proved illusory. The painful truth is that in 1972, Presidential candidates either are taking the black vote for granted or, worse, they just don't give a damn.

3. Harriet Tubman, 1849, *"I was the conductor of the Underground Railroad for eight years, and I can say what most conductors can't say. I never ran a train off the track and I never lost a passenger."* Harriet Tubman was an Underground Railroad activist, civil rights Black female and an abolitionist.

   Harriet Tubman emerged as the dominant historical symbol of Black resistance to slavery and she has been embraced, memorialized, commemorated, and championed by Americans from the late 19th century to the present. Tubman's representations changed over time and were captured by various segments of American society. Harriet Tubman, the warrior, was a popular image from the late 1850's into the Civil War, where she was allowed to ride at the head of Colonel James Montgomery's troops, and later led a squad of Black spies on reconnaissance missions from the Union Army. With the coming of Jim Crow and heightened white male chauvinism, most Americans in the mainstream forgot about Harriet Tubman, but African Americans did not. She is often depicted as the Underground Railroad Conductor, and "Black Moses" or as the demanding "General Tubman."

4. Sojourner Truth,1826, was an African American female abolitionist and women's rights activist. She was the first Black woman to sue a white man in a United States court and won in 1828. Sojourner Truth was the first Black woman to be honored with a bust in the U.S. Capitol. The bust was unveiled on April 28, 2009 and signed in order by former President George W. Bush on December 6, 2006.

   Sojourner Truth's famous speech entitled, "Ain't I a Woman?" delivered at the 1851 Women's Convention in Akron, Ohio she said,

   *"Well, children, where there is so much racket there must be something out of kilter. I think that 'twixt the Negroes of the South and the women at the North, all talking about rights, the white men will be in a fix pretty soon. But what's all this here talking about?*

*That man over there says that women need to be helped into carriages, and lifted over ditches, and to have the best place everywhere. Nobody ever helps me into carriages, or over mud-puddles, or gives me any best place! And ain't I a woman? Look at me! Look at my arm! I have ploughed and planted, and gathered into barns, and no man could head me! And ain't I a woman? I could work as much and eat as much as a man—when I could get it—and bear the lash as well! And ain't I a woman? I have borne thirteen children and seen most all sold off to slavery, and when I cried out with my mother's grief, none but Jesus heard me! And ain't I a woman?*

*Then they talk about this thing in the head; what's this they call it? [member of the audience whispers, "intellect"] That's it, honey. What's that got to do with women's rights or Negroes' rights? If my cup won't hold but a pint, and yours holds a quart, wouldn't you be mean not to let me have my little half measure full?*

*Then that little man in black there, he says women can't have as much rights as men, 'cause Christ wasn't a woman! Where did your Christ come from? Where did your Christ come from? From God and a woman! Man had nothing to do with Him.*

*If the first woman God ever made was strong enough to turn the world upside down all alone, these women together ought to be able to turn it back, and get it right side up again! And now they is asking to do it. The men better let them.*

*Obliged to you for hearing me, and now old Sojourner ain't got nothing more to say."*

In 2022, 196 years after Sojourner Truth started her fight for women's rights in 1826, women are still struggling for their rights, especially Black and brown women. These women paved the way for Black, brown and white women to achieve politically. They were pioneers, abolitionists, civil rights leaders, educators, religious leaders and entrepreneurs. Sojourner Truth in 1826, Harriet Tubman in 1849, Fannie Lou Hamer in 1964, Shirley Chisholm in 1968, all were Black women activists and civil rights leaders who fought for women's rights.

These 4 women had a great deal in common, i.e., strong will; a fighter; visionary; a belief in God; risk-taker; fearless; and a strong supporter of women's rights. They faced racism and sexism daily during their struggles fighting for justice for women especially Black and brown women. African American women played a key role in the American Civil Rights Movement, from a historical perspective. Without their struggle for freedom and justice, it would not have been possible for African Americans and people of color to achieve some symbol of racial justice. However, African American women were never given the necessary credit that they deserved because of racism and sexism. Unfortunately, the battles these women had to fight for over 150 years are still relevant today.

# CHAPTER 4

## AN ABBREVIATED HISTORICAL PERSPECTIVE OF A SLAVE, REVEREND WILLIAM RUSH-PLUMMER, THE FOUNDING FATHER OF FREDERICK DOUGLASS COMMUNITY, CHURCHES AND SCHOOLS IN MEMPHIS, TENNESSEE

## REV. WILLIAM RUSH-PLUMMER, BORN 1858, DIED 1930.

The author paraphrased some of the written information printed by AOL search document, April 28, 2008, highlighting contributions of Rev. William Rush-Plummer to the Frederick Douglass community. The writer expanded and updated events pertaining to the Frederick Douglass community, schools, churches and businesses.

I have updated the name of "Douglass" throughout this chapter to its real name after the great orator and abolitionist, "Frederick Douglass". This was done from an historical perspective to orientate and educate African American people of their "true" and enriched history. It is important for Black people to research their rich history and share it with Black, brown and white people. Then they can understand and appreciate the many great contributions Black people made in the United States. This will enlighten future generations to clearly acknowledge that Black people are pioneers in creating communities, schools, businesses, families and churches, even as a <u>slave,</u> named <u>William Rush-Plummer did.</u>

I've noted during my research that William Rush-Plummer, a slave, was bestowed by his slave master (his father) 40 acres of land and a mule, where the Frederick Douglass neighborhood currently stands. He donated his land to the community and named it after Frederick Douglass, a man he had come to befriend and admire. Therefore, historically, the community, churches and schools were originally named Frederick Douglass. Our schools and community represent the historical contribution of the founding father, a former slave, Reverend William Rush-Plummer. He was born in 1858 and died in 1930. Rev. Rush-Plummer took his 40 acres of land and turned it into a community, schools and churches, then named them after Frederick Douglass, an abolitionist and orator. He named the community, churches and schools, the Frederick Douglass community, Frederick Douglass churches and the Frederick Douglass schools. The St. Paul Frederick Douglass Missionary Baptist Church in 1902 was founded by Rev. William Rush-Plummer and he served as the first pastor in the Frederick Douglass Community.

I realize it is extremely difficult to change attitudes and mindsets that we were taught to believe for years, but we must make a concerted effort to learn and teach our real history. Ironically, we still have the descendants of Rev. Rush-Plummer living in the Frederick Douglass Community and throughout the city of Memphis and Shelby County, Tennessee. I have noted that after receiving information from Reverend William

Rush Plummer's family members that Mrs. Rosalind Jones-Burnett was the great-granddaughter of Reverend Plummer. Reverend Plummer's grandson named Solomon was Mrs. Rosalind Jones-Burnett's mother's father. Mrs. Burnett's mother's name was Beatrice Plummer-Jones. Mrs. Beatrice Plummer-Jones served as the treasurer of the Frederick Douglass PTA for many years and was extremely active in the Frederick Douglass community. She was born in 1908 and died in 1956.

Reverend William Rush-Plummer was born into a life of slavery in the Southern States in America. He was the only son of a white slave master, William Rush Sr. and his mother, a slave from Africa. Mrs. Rush demanded of her husband, that young William Rush Jr. not be given the Rush family name. As a result, William Rush Senior, modified his son's name giving him a hyphenated last name. William Jr. was renamed, William Rush-Plummer.

Slavery in the South was eventually abolished. When that time arrived, slaves were promised 40 acres and a mule. Although many newly freed slaves did not receive the promise at that time, William Rush Sr. gave (his son) William Rush-Plummer 40 acres in North Memphis, Tennessee. He turned his land into a community and named it after Fredrick Douglass. William Rush-Plummer was ordained in his young adult years and began to develop the land now known as the Frederick Douglass Community in Memphis, Tennessee after his family was released from slavery. Now referred to as Reverend Plummer, he had a strong resemblance to his father and a similar proper speech pattern (with a heavy southern dialect). He began opening many churches on his land including St. Paul Frederick Douglass Missionary Baptist Church (Need More Missionary Baptist Church), St. Stephens MB Church, St. John MB Church, St. Charles MB Church and at least three other local churches that were later sold to local Pastors and their congregations. From the very beginning, Christianity played a vital role in the Plummer family and the lives of families in the Frederick Douglass Community due to Reverend William Rush-Plummer's vision. In 1900, Reverend William Rush Plummer and his associates had a vision that a church was needed for the community. Under a bush arbor in Frederick Douglass Park, the first church known as "Need More" was established. Reverend Plummer, known as "Father Plummer" deliberately gave the church this name because he felt it needed more of everything: shelter, chairs, and people.

Saint Paul Frederick Douglass Missionary Baptist Church in 1902, 'Need More Church' moved to a new location for worship on Ellington Street and was given a new name, "Saint Paul Frederick Douglass Missionary Baptist Church". Reverend Plummer served as the church's first official pastor. He was succeeded by Reverend Bolton, followed by Reverend Anderson. The church moved in 1905 to its present location at 1543 Brookins Street. Memphis, Tennessee.

Rev. J.E. Ferguson became the fourth pastor of the church on the third Sunday in June 1931. Realizing that education had to be perpetuated in the community, Saint Paul Frederick Douglass Missionary Baptist Church allowed Frederick Douglass High School to hold classes in the early 1900s when the school was blown away by the "Great Storm". In 1935, the school burned to the ground and once again, Saint Paul Frederick Douglass Missionary Baptist Church opened its doors. Rev. Ferguson permitted the school to hold classes under the leadership of Mrs. Susie Crawford, principal and later Mr. Lucky Sharpe until the new school was built the following year. To further serve the community, Saint Paul was, also, used as a social center for feeding the poor. Rev. Ferguson served as pastor of Saint Paul Frederick Douglass Missionary Baptist Church for 60 years until his death on April 16, 1991.

Reverend Harry Davis was elected as Pastor, on the first Sunday in July in 1991 and is currently the Pastor. Under his leadership, Saint Paul Frederick Douglass Missionary Baptist Church, was re-documented under the name of Saint Paul Frederick Douglass Missionary Baptist Church under the direction of Reverend Harry Davis and is a landmark in the "Historic Frederick Douglass Community."

Over the years, through several generations, the name 'Rush' began to fade. New generations unaware of the family's history simply stopped using the full last name in the mid-1900s. Today the Plummer family seldom uses the name Rush, unless historical matters are being discussed. The Plummer family's official last name, although it may not show up on their birth certificates, is Rush-Plummer.

Church of the Living God, Missionary Baptist Church Pastor Maggie-Judith A. Fluker-Campbell, (Pastor Maggie Campbell) is the great-great granddaughter of Reverend William Rush-Plummer. She was the granddaughter of Reverend Plummer's daughter, Evangelist Maggie Plummer-Trout whose husband was Willie Trout Sr.

Evangelist Maggie Plummer insisted on the day Pastor Maggie Campbell was born that she be named after her. When her mother, Evelyn Fluker-Williams refused, initially naming her Judith A. Fluker, Plummer wrote the name Maggie in the margin of the birth certificate form followed by a dash next to the name Judith, which led to her first name to this day as Maggie-Judith. Her mother Evelyn Fluker-Williams and her father Willie [Plummer] Trout Jr. never changed it.

Pastor Maggie Campbell has been a member of Saint Paul Frederick Douglass Missionary Baptist Church since birth. She was baptized at the church at the approximate age of 12 years. She was trained by her grandmother and members of her family in Evangelism since her teen years. She accepted the calling on her life at the age of 13 years while attending Saint Paul Frederick Douglass Missionary Baptist Church under the late Reverend J. E. Ferguson.

Pastor Maggie Campbell left Memphis in 1985 and established residence in California while serving on active-duty as a member in the United States Navy where she had the opportunity to travel around the world. She established her first ministry in support of women and children in 1993 in Northern California.

Pastor Maggie Campbell lives in Southern California. She re-established her membership with Saint Paul Frederick Douglass Missionary Baptist Church and officially established an official covenant partnership between Saint Paul Frederick Douglass Missionary Baptist Church and her California-based Maggie Campbell Ministries on December 18, 2005. She became the first woman in her family's history to become an ordained Pastor. She was ordained on Friday, October 13, 2006 in Southern California. Shortly after her ordination Pastor Maggie Campbell and her husband, Alvin Campbell established a new church in Palmdale, California and dedicated it to her great grandfather, the late Reverend William Rush-Plummer called, 'Church of the Living God', www.church-living-god.org on February 4, 2009. They have continued their affiliation and ministry partnership with Saint. Paul Frederick Douglass Missionary Baptist Church. Alvin and Pastor Maggie Campbell opened the 'Church of the Living God' (Missionary Baptist) in memory of Pastor Maggie's great-great grandfather Reverend Rush-Plummer where Women in Ministry Leadership receive specialized training and Official Ordination with a goal to plan more churches to continue to edify the Word of God.

The Missionary Baptist Association established In September 2010, Pastor Maggie Campbell established the "Missionary Baptist Association" (MBA), in support of Women in Ministry Leadership. One of the purposes the MBA, is to bring together churches with like faith and aspirations to fellowship with one another within the MBA in California and nationwide. This was to encourage non-denominational churches to join with the Missionary Baptist church family to organize retreats and reunions as well. The Missionary Baptist Association later became the "Annual Women's Conference" which is held annually in May between Mother's Day and Memorial Day.

The Annual Women's Conference welcomes women of all ages, religious backgrounds and non-religious affiliations. The purpose: To aid women in healing and to deal with the adversities of everyday life. The Women's Conference, through the Church of the Living God (CLG) strives to inspire, motivate, educate and support women including with their education and career aspirations. CLG believe women should support one another's efforts, goals and aspirations. Mature women should reach out to the younger women to help teach them life skills and the younger women should embrace our mature women who are full of wisdom to help lead and guide them along the way.

The Women's Conference covers the topics that are important to women that are oftentimes not discussed in Church services such as, but not limited to: Forgiveness, the Power of Prayer, Alternative Lifestyles, Sex outside of Marriage, Pro-life / Pro-choice issues, God's Covenant of Healing, Entrepreneurship, personal and professional growth, women in ministry leadership and much more. No one understands the issues of women more than other women. The Women's Conference includes 3 days of praise, worship, inspirational music, pastoral sermons, motivational speakers, musical celebrations, fellowship, networking opportunities for women, breakfast, receptions and dinner.

The Church of the Living God and its affiliate churches and ministries collectively congratulated, Pastor Maggie Campbell on her acceptance of the Call to the Office of Bishop on May 7, 2013. Hereinafter, she was officially addressed as, "Bishop Maggie Campbell".

Bishop Campbell worked hard - following in her great grandfather's footsteps Reverend William Rush-Plummer for more than 10 years to equip many women and some men to succeed in ministry. She has continued to work for years as the Overseer of churches and ministries, have helped graduates to plan new churches in New York, Tennessee and California. She has staffed many existing churches in the Antelope Valley in California and several locations outside of the State with newly ordained, trained and equipped Women of God. As the professor over the, 'Women in Ministry Leadership Training Institute', Bishop Campbell have taught women who are now Pastors, Ministers, Evangelists and Missionaries; several of which are senior pastors or associate pastors at churches in the Antelope Valley as well as various cities across the United States. She is the first female Pastor in her family of male pastors dating back to the 1800s and is therefore now the first woman to be Called to the Office of Bishop in her family. The duties and responsibilities of which she is required to do, she has been doing for many years prior to her official acceptance date of May 7, 2013. Bishop Campbell's new status opens the doors for many Women in Ministry across the country and within the Rush-Plummer and Fluker families. She is obviously an intelligent woman with multiple gifts that she uses to continue to edify the Word of God and for the Body of Christ. A role model to women and teen girls, she is a Woman of God who has put in an extreme amount of hard work. She has shown qualities that she openly shares with all Women in Ministry who are willing, ready and able to do what God has called them to do as well. Bishop Campbell's dedication and perseverance has manifested itself into one of the best 'Women in Ministry Leadership Training Institutes' in America. It continues to grow each year. We all should be proud of her. Many women seek her guidance and the opportunity to train within the programs she teaches because they know she will give more than 100% of herself to making sure they receive what they need to succeed. It all began in the Frederick Douglass Community in Memphis, Tennessee - Founded by her great grandfather, William Rush-Plummer.

The Frederick Douglass community is home to Frederick Douglass Elementary School on Ash Street. Since the school was built through the early 1970, the Frederick Douglass community also had a Junior High School for grades 7 - 9 as well as a high school grades 10 - 12. In the mid-1970s students passing from the 6th grade into Junior high were bussed to Gragg Junior High School on Jackson Avenue and later to Craigmont High

School with the option of returning to Frederick Douglass High School when they entered the 10th grade. Not all students returned to Frederick Douglass High School. Many remained at Craigmont High School in North Memphis, Raleigh community.

The first city championship of any sport at Frederick Douglass High School was the 1960 Men's Basketball team. The coach was William (Bill) Little. (Bill) Little. Team members and team trainer were:

1. John Rhodes      5. Maurice Tucker
2. Robert Manning   6. Willie Kimmons **
3. Jack Ballad      7. Joseph Norman      9. William Hudson
4. Odell King       8. William Brown      10. Johnny Rudd, Trainer

Frederick Douglass High School won its second basketball championship in 1973. The original Frederick Douglass High School served the neighborhood in 1938. It burned to the ground and resumed meeting at the church (Need More) the first of six churches founded by Rev. William Rush-Plummer. The next school was built in place of the damaged one and used from 1946 to 1981 when it was closed. The building was listed on the National Register of Historic Places in 1998. The new Frederick Douglass High School was opened 27 years later in 2008. Dr. Carol Johnson, superintendent of schools; Mrs. Sara Lewis, Chairperson of the Memphis City School Board and Mr. Carl Johnson, Vice Chair, along with other community leaders were instrumental in approving Mrs. Janet Ware Thompson, as its first principal. She was a 1975 graduate of Frederick Douglass High School. Dr. Johnson appointed Mrs. Thompson to the principalship. Afterwards, Dr. Johnson assumed the superintendent's position in Boston, Massachusetts. Mr. Dan Ward, a long-time teacher and administrator in Memphis City Schools was asked to accept the position as interim superintendent. The Memphis City School Board approved the appointment and Mr. Ward accepted it.

Today, it is one of the oldest but newest Memphis City Schools, with a state-of-the-art 1,500-seat varsity gym, a 1,100-seat auditorium, a football field (with a track) in the middle of Frederick Douglass Park, and baseball field at the northeast corner of Frederick Douglass Park. The Community Recreation Center is located behind the new Frederick Douglass High School where the original Negro golf course was located.

Hopefully, this brief and modified historical perspective has shed some light on a slave, Rev. William Rush-Plummer's outstanding contributions as the founding father of the Frederick Douglass community, schools and churches.

It was also noted that Rev. Plummer's tremendous foresight and vision paved the way for his great-granddaughter, Pastor Maggie Campbell, to become the first woman in her family's history to be ordained as a pastor. This reminds me that Mr. Max Holder, Mrs. Chisholm's mentor, made it possible for her to be elected as the first Black woman to the U.S. Congress in 1968. In1972, Max Holder and others were instrumental in Mrs. Chisholm becoming the first Black woman to seek the office of the presidency of the United States of America.

*Congresswoman Shirley Chisholm*

# CHAPTER 5

## SHIRLEY CHISHOLM'S PERSONAL LIFE, FIRST AND SECOND MARRIAGES AND HER ADOPTED GODSON

Shirley Anita St. Hill met and married Conrad Chisholm in 1949. She thought an early marriage to Conrad would give her a way out of the pain and agony from a family that failed her. Throughout her entire life, she never forgave the family.

Conrad Chisholm was from Jamaica. In the United States he worked as a private investigator that featured lawsuits concerning negligence. Later in the marriage, he became Mrs. Chisholm's chauffeur. Ironically, she never learned how to drive. As she mentioned to me several times, that her first husband, Conrad Chisholm, who was 8 years older, intentionally didn't teach her how to drive. This was his way of controlling her daily schedule. It was obvious that Conrad was somewhat jealous of Mrs. Chisholm and extremely intimidated by her success in life. Mrs. Chisholm loved children and she mentioned to me that Conrad couldn't produce children because of a stated health condition he shared with her early in their marriage. She believed him and decided to try and keep the marriage alive and healthy. One day while at home in Brooklyn, New York, Mrs. Chisholm called me and stated that a young man came to the door and asked for his father, Conrad Chisholm. Mrs. Chisholm was terrified, angry and thoroughly upset because Conrad had lied to her about being unable to have children. He knew she desperately wanted children even though she experienced the personal pain of at least two miscarriages. This was one of the reasons she asked me to be her godson.

During many conversations with Mrs. Chisholm, she said she married Arthur Hardwick in the same year she divorced Conrad Chisholm because Conrad was totally controlling from the beginning of their marriage. He was 33 years old and Mrs. Chisholm was 25. She often told me that Conrad had another family in Jamaica and he also had a son.

Mrs. Chisholm and her first husband, Conrad, met while she was running from one community meeting to another. She was young and vibrant and interested in making a better life for Black and brown people and especially women. As a young student in undergraduate and graduate schools, she noticed all the racial and gender bias teachings her father had shared with her about this country.

Conrad Chisholm was employed by the City of New York and early on in their marriage he was a private investigator and a licensed chauffeur. Mrs. Chisholm and Conrad spent a great deal of time away from each other. I'm sure this had some effect on the marriage over the years. She was so busy and there was very little time for the two of them early on in their marriage and throughout their 28 years of marriage to really get to know each other. Mrs. Chisholm was a young, charismatic, talkative 25-year-old. Conrad was a seasoned, sophisticated and controlling 33-year-old man. He knew how to do the things that Mrs. Chisholm would want and need and he certainly knew how to say and do the things that would make her feel wanted, needed and feel good. Conrad's investigation experience and being a chauffeur in New York put him in an excellent position to monitor and control everything Mrs. Chisholm did. She didn't drive nor had time to concentrate on anything other than her community and political events which by now were enormous and time-consuming.

Mrs. Chisholm said to me that Conrad never mentioned that he had a family in Jamaica and he certainly didn't tell her that he had a child in Brooklyn, New York. It is obvious that he took advantage of young Shirley Chisholm at the age of 25. Also, she didn't have many men interested in dating her or took any serious interest in her as a girlfriend. Conrad detected this immediately which is why he pursued her aggressively. He was smooth and persistent while winning her over. He gave her all the attention she longed for and really needed and desired.

Conrad refused to teach her how to drive and reassured her that he was interested in her political career by becoming actively involved with her campaigns. Mrs. Chisholm felt extremely excited about all of this attention and truly misunderstood Conrad's motives. She so desperately needed to be loved and desired lots of male attention. Conrad was in total control and Mrs. Chisholm appreciated and admired all the attention Conrad was giving her. But later on, near the end of the 28-year marriage, Mrs.

Chisholm realized that Conrad not only controlled her life, but deprived her of having children with all these lies. After 28 years with Conrad, she is now 53 years old and it is probably not possible to have a child. She was totally drained mentally and physically and realized Conrad had wasted 28 years of her life, certainly her reproductive years. It is unfortunate that it took 28 years for Mrs. Chisholm to realize the true reality of her marriage. Many in the media believed that Conrad had her best interest at heart and had invested his time making her successful in the community and in the political arena. This was the public side of Mrs. Chisholm and she always made a concerted effort to protect her private life from the public. She knew how vicious and dangerous people in the media and politics could be. She had witnessed, first hand, many politicians destroyed by them.

Mrs. Chisholm had known Arthur Hardwick during their days in the New York State Assembly where they had both served from 1964-1968. Mrs. Chisholm immediately divorced Conrad in 1977 and in a very short period of time, in the same year 1977, she married Arthur Hardwick. Art probably saved her life, certainly saved her from all the pain she was enduring from 28 years of lies after being married to Conrad. I don't think she ever recovered from her long disappointing ordeal with Conrad Chisholm. Arthur Hardwick was a great savior for her stability and peace of mind. Arthur Hardwick, now a widower from his first wife, never had any children before he married Mrs. Chisholm. Now she is 53 years old and Arthur was 61 years old.

In addition to her terrible experience with first husband, and because of her strong relationship with her father, her mother and the 3 sisters were extremely jealous and this is when Mrs. Chisholm became estranged from her family. Also, the death of her father who left only her some money in a savings account, and not the 3 sisters, intensified even more the rift between the family. Her mother and the 3 sisters often said that their father cared more about Shirley than anyone else in the family. This, also, furthered the rift in the family that really never healed. Once again, she was alone and really relying on her new husband, Arthur Hardwick for some moral support and protection.

Arthur Hardwick's first wife had passed and Mrs. Chisholm's father had died. Mrs. Chisholm was too embarrassed to share relationship troubles with her first husband, Conrad, but later shared them with me.

This is why she married her second husband, Arthur Hardwick, Jr. in 1977, shortly after she divorced her first husband, Conrad Chisholm. She was married to Conrad from 1949 to 1977. Arthur Hardwick, Jr., born in Augusta, Georgia was a successful businessman. He served as the first African American Assemblyman to represent the 143rd District of Buffalo, New York. Mrs. Chisholm and Arthur Hardwick met in the New York Assembly as representatives in Albany where they both served from 1964 to 1968. Later, during their marriage, Mr. Hardwick sustained serious injuries in an automobile accident in 1982, so Mrs. Chisholm announced one of the reasons she was retiring from politics in 1983 was to nurse her husband back to health. Neither marriage produced any children.

I was adopted as the son she never had. Mrs. Chisholm always made a concerted effort to protect her true feelings and her personal and private life. Many times, through the years, we would talk on the phone and she would be crying uncontrollably for most of our phone conversations. She often would speak with my mother in Memphis, Tennessee because they both had endured many disappointments in life with men. Mrs. Chisholm and my mother were in the same age range and she knew she could trust my mother and me since I had met her many years ago as a student in the 3rd grade in Memphis, Tennessee. My mother jokingly said to Mrs. Chisholm that my son, Willie, was the oldest of 16 sisters and 11 brothers, and Mrs. Chisholm could have me as her godson. My mother had 9 children by my stepfather and my father had 18 children by other women. My mother and father were never married. I thought my mother was joking, but I didn't think it was funny at the time, especially as an 8 or 9- year-old child. I asked myself, "Was mother really going to give me away?" Today, many years later, as I think about it, it was a great thought, even though my mother was only joking with Mrs. Chisholm at the time. The Lord works in a mysterious way in bringing people together. As the years passed, Mrs. Chisholm and I kept in contact with each other and reconnected once again, in person, in the early 70's. We remained in regular contact until her death. She spoke at every college and university where I was employed.

My mother would visit me in Washington, D.C. I was Dean of the College of Education and Human Ecology, University of the District of Columbia (UDC), during the time Mrs. Chisholm was in Congress.

Mrs. Chisholm served as my facilitator of the Shirley Chisholm's Summer Institute for the College of Education. After seeing all the pain and suffering, through the years, that Mrs. Chisholm endured as well as my mother, I had made a personal promise to myself. I would go to school and get a good education and try to make mother and Mrs. Chisholm be proud of me. By the Grace of God and hard work, I was able to succeed in life as one with a doctorate degree at the age of 28. I served in many teaching and administrative positions at Black and white colleges and universities as a college professor, a college dean, vice president, president and chancellor.

In 1977, Mrs. Chisholm mentioned to me that St. Francis College in Brooklyn, New York had a dean's position open and told me to apply. I applied and was fortunate enough to get the Dean's position. During my first week at the College, I noticed that St. Francis was a former Catholic monastery college and white. This was an interesting experience for me since I am Black, a Baptist and from the south.

Mrs. Chisholm made several speaking engagements at St. Francis College during my tenure at the College. She stated that St. Francis College had no Blacks teaching nor holding administrative positions and urged the President to hire some Blacks at the College. I was the only Black face working at the College in any position in 1977. I thank God for Mrs. Chisholm's influence and her continued support.

I am Dr. Willie J. Greer Kimmons, the adopted godson of the late, great Honorable Shirley Chisholm. I've been around Mrs. Chisholm for most of my life. I first met her in Memphis, Tennessee where she was speaking to the local NAACP Organizational Conference. The local Memphis NAACP was then under the leadership of the late Dr. Rev. Benjamin Hooks, the first Black judge in Shelby County, Tennessee. His wife, Mrs. Frances Hooks was my 3rd grade teacher. Mrs. Chisholm was also asked to speak to Mrs. Hooks' 3rd grade class where I was a student. Mrs. Hooks said, "Willie Kimmons, since you loved to talk, I want you to introduce the guest speaker for today, Mrs. Shirley Chisholm, and I did. I remember Mrs. Chisholm asking me how old I was. When I told her I was 8, she asked how many brothers and sisters I had. I told her I didn't know because my father and mother were not married. She told me she had always wanted children and that she loved children. She continued to say that maybe one day she would adopt me. I just smiled, said thank you and that I would ask my mother. Mrs. Chisholm thought my response was funny and that was the beginning of a life-long relationship between Mrs. Chisholm and me.

Years later, after having received my PhD. Degree, and authoring 5 books, Dr. Rev. Hooks would ask me several times to speak and conduct book signings of my 5th book, <u>A Parenting Guidebook</u> at his church, Greater Middle Baptist Church, in Memphis, Tennessee. The guidebook is for families, schools, teachers, churches and communities in assisting parents with rearing their children. Dr. Hooks' wife, Mrs. Frances Hooks, was the choir director and my former 3rd grade teacher. I was sitting in the pulpit next to Rev. Hooks, with my back to the choir, Mrs. Hooks tapped me on my head to say, "Willie Kimmons, I want you to do a good job." She was always teaching and encouraging me as if I was still in her 3rd grade class. At the time I was 33 years old.

In the 1970's, Dr. Hooks became the National President of the NAACP, when the national organization moved to New York where I served as dean of St. Francis College in 1977, which was near Mrs. Chisholm's Congressional District. In 1979, former borough president of Brooklyn, New York, The Honorable Howard Golden and Mrs. Chisholm honored me as an outstanding educator, public servant and community leader while I was working in Brooklyn, New York at St. Francis College.

*My godmother,*
*Congresswoman*
*Shirley Chisholm and me*
*Having fun*

From that brief meeting many years ago in Memphis, Tennessee, Mrs. Chisholm and I became close. I was the son that she never had the opportunity to produce in life. She has been a presenter and speaker at every institution where I have been employed as a classroom teacher, college professor, college dean, vice president, president and chancellor.

Once again, Mrs. Chisholm encouraged me to write my 5th book, <u>A Parenting Guidebook</u> which is for parents, grandparents, teachers, schools, churches, families and communities to assist in raising their children. Mrs. Chisholm wrote the foreword to my book.

In my home here in Daytona Beach, Florida, I have a special place in my house that's called the "Shirley Chisholm Room"; and she had a room in her Ormond Beach, Florida home named "The Willie's Room". I assisted Mrs. Chisholm to relocate to Florida. In 1991 while she lived in Palm Coast, Florida, I would come down every summer and spend about 10 days with her to get away from the stress of my duties as a college administrator. For the last 4 years of her life here in Florida, she and I would go to lunch and dinner at least 3 days a week in Daytona Beach, Florida. I would be her personal driver for everyday chores from doctor appointments, to beauty and nail salons, other errands and sometimes church services. We would often read books and discuss current events on political, religious and civil rights issues. During these times, she very seldom discussed her family.

After her second husband, Arthur Hardwick, died, Mrs. Chisholm asked me to assist her, as her adopted godson, to dispose of all the items in the Williamsville, New York home. The large house consumed the entire cul-de-sac. In the basement were 8 large freezers of meat and food. Arthur always stated that since he grew up poor in Georgia, he would never be poor without any material things again in life. There were enough canned goods and other food items in the house that could last them for years. The house was divided into two sections. Art had one side and Mrs. Chisholm had the other and they would meet in the middle of this huge house on the weekend. Art had a small golf "putting green" on his side and Mrs. Chisholm had a massive library and reading room on her side of the house.

Arthur had over 100 custom-made suits, many he had never worn and 200 or more custom designed shirts, and half of them had never been out of the original packages. He had over 100 pairs of shoes, 50 or more overcoats, top coats, 30 umbrellas and at least 100 neckties. After Arthur's death in 1986, it took months for Mrs. Chisholm to give all these things away to various community and charitable organizations. Unfortunately, Art's clothes were too small for me to wear. There were numerous garage sales at their house in Williamsville, New York every weekend. It took months to get rid of all the clothes, furniture, food and other items in the large house which was part of my assigned job.

One of the saddest days of my life was attending Mrs. Chisholm's 2nd husband's funeral in Buffalo, New York. After the heart-wrenching experience of losing her father (which created the rift between her mother and the 3 sisters), the 2nd disappointment was with Conrad, her first husband of 28 years. She mentioned to me several times that Conrad had a family in Jamaica during their marriage, that she didn't know about. Mrs. Chisholm felt she was once again all alone. Arthur Hardwick's funeral and the private repast at their home in Williamsville, New York, a suburb of Buffalo, was long, highly emotional and sad. This was one of the first times I witnessed Mrs. Chisholm in real pain. I was concerned about her health and state of mind. For years she had been estranged from her family. She lost her father and two husbands. Now, as a private person with very few real friends, Mrs. Chisholm found herself all alone. I tried to assist her in any way I could by calling her almost daily and visiting her on a regular basis at the home in Williamsville. During one of my visits, "Mrs. C" mentioned to me that she was learning to drive and parallel parking so she could pick me up from the airport. The next time I came to visit her,

I waited 30-40 minutes for her to pick me up. Finally, I called her. She shouted through the phone, "Willie, damn it! I don't drive at night. You better get a cab. Bye!" Mrs. Chisholm never learned to drive!

In 1991, Mrs. Chisholm moved to Palm Coast, Florida, then to Ormond Beach, Florida, which was closer to where I lived in Daytona Beach. We had special lunches or dinners every Monday, Wednesday and Friday. We were always joined by her friend and my mentor, the late Mr. Charles Cherry, Sr. He was the former city commissioner, local and state president of the NAACP. And owner of the Black radio station and local Black newspaper. Mr. Cherry had a weekly radio program called, "Express Yourself". Frequently, Mrs. Chisholm and I were guest hosts. After the radio program, the three of us would go to lunch and spend some quality time together discussing civil rights, political and educational issues. During these sessions, I learned a great deal about politics and life.

One day in June 2003, while we were at our weekly lunch, I noticed that Mrs. Chisholm was extremely tired. She went to the women's room at the restaurant 3 or 4 times during our meal. The last time Mrs. Chisholm went to the restroom, she stayed over 20 minutes. I knew this wasn't normal, so I asked our waitress to check on her for me. The waitress came running out of the women's room screaming that Mrs. Chisholm was lying on the floor. I immediately asked the restaurant manager to call for an ambulance. The EMT's arrived within 10 minutes. We spent the next 30 minutes pleading with Mrs. Chisholm, trying to convince her to go to the hospital and get medically checked out. I knew how vain and private she was, but she stated in a loud voice, "Willie, I don't need to go to the hospital. I'm ok, I just need some rest." The EMT's said that they could not force her to go to the hospital. They did a quick routine check on her and in the next 40 minutes, Mrs. Chisholm was signing autographs and taking pictures with EMT personnel, and a number of people in the restaurant. Immediately after this event, I took Mrs. Chisholm to her home in Ormond Beach, Florida, about 25 minutes away.

I have been a diabetic since 2002 and noticed similar symptoms around this same time that Mrs. Chisholm was experiencing them; sleeping most of the day, always tired, not being able to focus and easily irritated. She ate any and everything she wanted and was not watching the kind of food she was eating. As her adopted godson, I tried on numerous occasions to take her to a diabetic doctor for a thorough check up. Once again "Mrs. C", as I called her, scolded me saying, "Willie, I'm fine. I just need some rest." After more than 20 years of doing research on diabetes and conducting workshops around the country, I realized that Mrs. Chisholm probably died from having a series of diabetic strokes. I'm in constant pain and feeling guilty for being out of town on speaking engagements and book signings when she passed away. The medical doctors listed her death as a series of strokes. Now, I think those were probably diabetic strokes and she never recovered.

"Mrs. C" was such a public figure in life, that before she could leave her house for a dental appointment, grocery shopping, to the bank, or any place in public, I had to take her to the beauty salon to get her hair and nails done before she went anywhere. So, I became her personal chauffer and would drive her to these places because she never learned how to drive and neither of her two husbands took the time to teach her. Even before her 2nd husband, Art, died, he had purchased a new car for her which she never drove. It still had plastic covers over the seats and never had used the radio.

After each trip to the bank, beauty shop, nail shop and grocery store, she would take 2 to 3 hours talking, taking pictures and signing autographs with people. I would wait in my car until she called for me. Always, from grocery shopping, she would bring me cookies! Mrs. C never thought I would grow up. She was so private and always on display as a public figure. She had concerns through the years about how people perceived her as a Black female elected official. Mrs. Chisholm was the type of person that never talked about life and death. I strongly believe that she thought she would never die.

On November 16, 2004, my mentor, Mr. Cherry passed. He would always say to Mrs. Chisholm and me that what he admired about being great friends with the two of us was that we didn't want "anything" from him, but his love and friendship. Two months later, January 1, 2005, Mrs. Chisholm died. I lost my two best friends, my mentors, advisors and an adopted godmother. God bless their souls.

I often reminiscence and cherish the wonderful years and time Mrs. Chisholm, my adopted godmother, and Mr. Cherry, my mentor, and I spent with each other. My on-going work is to publicly acknowledge Mrs. Chisholm's legacy and life as long as I am on this earth. I will be educating, orientating and informing people, young and old, Black, brown and white about the profound contributions Shirley Chisholm made in this country and the world. I truly miss her guidance, wisdom, intellect, honesty and presence. There will never be another Honorable Shirley Anita St. Hill Chisholm-Hardwick and no one can replace her.

"A Catalyst for Change", "Unbought and Unbossed", "The Good Fight", "Fighting Shirley" was the Honorable Shirley Anita St. Hill Chisholm-Hardwick's platform.

*The Honorable Shirley Chisholm and her adopted godson,*
*Dr. Willie J. Greer Kimmons*

# CHAPTER 6

# THE BEGINNING OF SHIRLEY CHISHOLM'S POLITICAL YEARS AND TO THE PRESIDENCY OF THE UNITED STATES OF AMERICA

The interest in pursuing a political career was introduced to Shirley early in her life by her father who saw how courageous and ambitious she was. Her college professors encouraged her to consider a political career, she replied that she faced a "double handicap" as both Black and female.

Mrs. Chisholm started her political career in 1953 with the advice of her mentor, Mr. Wesley McDonald Holder, (Max), known as the "Dean of Black Politics". Max and Shirley Chisholm actively campaigned for Mr. Lewis Flaff, Jr. to become the first Black judge in Brooklyn, New York. This led to her involvement in the Bedford-Stuyvesant Political League, a group that fought for economic empowerment and civil rights. From there, she participated other political groups, including the League of Women Voters, the Brooklyn Democratic Club and the Unity Democratic Club.

Initially, Mrs. Chisholm worked as a nursery school teacher, in 1949, she married Conrad Q. Chisholm, a private investigator (they divorced in 1977). She earned a master's degree from Columbia University in early childhood education in 1951. By 1960, she was a consultant to the New York City Division of Day Care. Ever aware of racial and gender inequality, she joined local chapters of the League of Women Voters, the National Association for the Advancement of Colored People (NAACP), the Urban League, as well as the Democratic Party club in Bedford-Stuyvesant, Brooklyn, New York.

In 1964, Mrs. Chisholm ran for and became the second African American in the New York state Legislature. After court-ordered redistricting created a new, heavily Democratic district in her neighborhood of Bedford-Stuyvesant in 1968 she sought -and won-a seat in Congress. There, "Fighting Shirley" introduced more than 50 pieces of legislation and championed racial and gender equality, the plight of the poor, and ending the Vietnam War. She was a co-founder of the National Women's Political Caucus in 1971 and in 1977 became the first Black woman and second woman ever to serve on the powerful House Rules Committee. That same year, 1977, Congresswoman Chisholm divorced Conrad Chisholm and married Arthur Hardwick, Jr., a New York State legislator and a businessman from Buffalo, New York.

Discrimination followed Chisholm's quest for the 1972 Democratic Party presidential nomination. She was blocked from participating in televised primary debates, and after taking legal action, was permitted to make just one speech. She entered 12 primaries and garnered 152 of the delegates' votes (10% of the total)-despite an under-financed campaign and contentiousness from the predominantly male Congressional Black Caucus. Still, students, women, and minorities followed the "Chisholm Trail".

Mrs. Chisholm entered the 91$^{st}$ Congress as a Freshman Congresswoman in 1969 and established herself as a force to be reckoned with. She was born to Barbados parents. They were long on discipline but strong on love. Her parents survived the depths of depression and poverty to give their children college educations. It was during these formative years she developed racial awareness and a resolve to do something concrete for the African American community. She was persistently challenging the inequities of the machine and came to be regarded as a trouble making maverick, but one to be reckoned with. Congresswoman Chisholm was a dynamic and fighting woman with an unswerving belief in her own purpose: to put the needs of her people before political expediency. After being elected in 1968 as the first African American woman in Congress. She won this unique designation the hard way---against the odds of her race and sex and against all the ground rules of the political game. Since her fiery, precedent-breaking first months in Congress, Mrs. Chisholm continued to work under this system bucking manner. Although she was not successful in her bid for the Presidency in 1972, her name, her ideas and her commitment became imbedded in Americans' consciousness. She earned praise for her efforts on behalf of Black/white colleges and universities, compensatory education, minimum wage for domestics, American Indians, the Haitian Refugees, migrant farm workers, and the poor. Congresswoman Chisholm's fierce individualism resulted in a reputation as "maverick" and "unpredictable". These terms indicated that she was a powerbroker in her own right in the House of Representatives.

Mrs. Chisholm stated 'that her greatest political asset which professional politicians fear, is my mouth, out of which comes all kinds of things one shouldn't always discuss for reasons of political expediency". Mrs. Chisholm hired only women for her staff, half of whom were African Americans. She stated that "of my two handicaps, being female put many more obstacles in my path than being Black." She often said, "ironically, her major headaches seem to come from Black politicians, especially males; they think that I am trying to take power from them, the Black man must step forward; but that doesn't mean the Black woman must step back; while they are rapping and snapping, "I'm mapping." Congresswoman Chisholm noted that "it is hard to imagine, in this era of sharp division in politics, the remarkable moment during her 1972 campaign when she visited her segregationist rival, Alabama Governor George Wallace in his hospital room after he was shot and wounded. "What are your people going to say?" Wallace asked her. "I know what they are going to say," she said. "But I wouldn't want what happened to you to happen to anyone." She recalled that her words moved him to tears. It would be difficult to overestimate the impact and influence of Mrs. Chisholm's Congressional service and Presidential Candidacy. While Congress today remains disproportionately white and male, one in five members of the current House and Senate are a racial or ethnic minority, making the current Congress the most diverse in history.

At Mrs. Chisholm's acclaimed speech on the Equal Right Amendment in 1970, she said, "The Constitution they wrote was designed to protect the rights of white male citizens. As there were no Black Founding Fathers, there were no founding mothers---a great pity on both counts. It is not too late to complete the work they left undone. Today, here, we should start to do this."

These are some of the reasons I pursued the political arena to carry out the advice that my father and mentors taught me about having political and economic power. We can protest, march, shout, sing and pray constantly, even though as a child of God, I truly believe in the power of prayer, but my Black and brown brothers and sisters, in addition to praying, you need some <u>real political power</u> and <u>real economic power.</u> It is important for us to be at the table where the real decisions are being made, vote and make a difference in your life and the lives of others. History provides abundant examples of people whose greatest gift was redeeming, inspiring, liberating and nurturing the gifts of others by voting.

*Congresswoman Chisholm with me, her adopted godson, at a political function in Washington, D.C.*

*Jet* magazine spoke with activists and elected officials from across the nation who described the upcoming election—the second since the passage of the Voting Rights Act of 1965 which bolstered the power of Black voters in the South—as a significant opportunity for an African-American candidate to pursue the presidency. Cleveland Mayor Carl Stokes—the brother of Representative Louis Stokes of Ohio—was confident that a Black man could win with the backing of "Black, brown, Chicano, poor white and marginal persons involved in the politics of coalition." *Jet* cited the results of an unscientific survey conducted by a Chicago radio station, which compiled a list of potential African-American candidates that included Senator Edward Brooke of Massachusetts, Representative John Conyers of Michigan, Georgia state representative Julian Bond, and Supreme Court Justice Thurgood Marshall. Only one woman received votes in this informal poll: the first Black woman elected to Congress, Representative Shirley Chisholm of New York.

A former teacher and New York state legislator, "Fighting" Shirley Chisholm had been in the spotlight since she arrived on Capitol Hill in

January 1969. In her first term in Congress, Chisholm boldly rejected her assignment to the Agriculture Committee and forced Democratic leaders to appoint her to the Veterans' Affairs Committee where she could better serve her Brooklyn constituents. Now in her second term, Shirley Chisholm was a founding member of the recently formed Congressional Black Caucus (CBC) and the only female. Congresswoman Chisholm was the only one from the CBC to boycott Nixon's State of the Union Address in January 1971 after the President refused to meet with the group. With a new seat on the influential House Education and Labor Committee, Chisholm was a formidable national politician by the summer of 1971.

On July 31, at the annual conference of the National Welfare Rights Organization, Chisholm indicated that she was exploring a run for the presidency. Wearing a yellow suit and a button bearing the slogan "Welfare Not Warfare"—a protest against America's military intervention in Vietnam—Chisholm embraced the idea that a diverse coalition of everyday people could create a popular movement that transcended the country's political status quo. African Americans, women, Latinos, antiwar activists, labor unions, students, poor people, and others sought someone to represent their interests, she noted. "We must have this coalition," Chisholm said. "This nation must be turned around." Amid thunderous applause, Chisholm remained on stage holding two fingers high above her head.

Chisholm formally announced her candidacy for president in January 1972 and worked to forge what she called a "union of the disenfranchised." With limited funding and a small staff, she used her platform to advocate for progressive causes and developed a strategy to win delegates in key presidential primaries; if need be, she was ready to continue her quest for the nomination into the July 1972 Democratic National Convention in Miami, Florida. But almost immediately, Chisholm faced opposition from other Democratic presidential hopefuls, prominent Black politicians, members of the CBC, and political rivals back home in her Brooklyn congressional district. Throughout the campaign, she dismissed criticism that her candidacy was self-serving or merely symbolic. "I am for real, and I am very serious about what I am doing.

What set Chisholm apart from the others, however, was her emphasis on the importance of women at the forefront of any coalition. In July 1971,

Chisholm, alongside Representatives <u>Bella Abzug</u> of New York and <u>Patsy T. Mink</u> of Hawaii, as well as Betty Friedan, Fannie Lou Hamer, Gloria Steinem, and other activists, attended the organizational meeting of the National Women's Political Caucus to discuss their electoral strategy for 1972. The organization called for the passage of an equal rights amendment to the Constitution, the election of more women to Congress—there were only 14 at the time—and a guarantee that women would comprise half of all delegates to both the Democratic and Republican conventions in 1972. If "women and minorities ever got together on issues and on their own tragic underrepresentation in the places of power . . . this country would never be the same," Chisholm told the group. She reminded the caucus that "no one gives away political power. It must be taken," she said, "and we will take it." She then paraphrased an excerpt from her hero, Frederick Douglass' speech, "Power concedes nothing without a demand, it never did and never will."

Other Democrats, however, worked to retain their power. On December 24, Mayor Lindsay invited Chisholm to his official residence on Manhattan's Upper East Side. Lindsay urged her to stand aside to avoid siphoning votes away from his own presidential campaign. Chisholm replied that McGovern had made a similar request, adding, "goddam it, this is the American Dream—the chance for a Black woman to run for the highest office." Chisholm told Lindsay she had a different idea. "Why don't you and McGovern get together—and one of you decide to back out?"

Chisholm formally announced her candidacy for president on January 24, 1972, at a Bedford-Stuyvesant school auditorium in her Brooklyn congressional district. Speaking to an enthusiastic crowd of about 500, she described her progressive campaign in broad terms and spoke about shattering the barriers of race and gender in presidential politics.

Chisholm knew she faced an uphill battle. Others in the Democratic primary had more than $1 million in their campaign accounts, but Chisholm had managed to raise only about $44,000. She also faced resistance from Black Members of Congress who criticized her for launching her campaign without the CBC's blessing. After Chisholm's announcement, however, <u>Ron Dellums</u> of California and <u>Parren Mitchell</u> of Maryland, both members of the CBC, endorsed her. Chisholm's strategy focused on winning several key primary states in the spring of 1972. She sought to amass "enough delegates to have clout" as a powerbroker at the convention in July, 1972.

Chisholm also planned to demand certain concessions from the winning Democratic candidate: naming a Black vice-presidential candidate to the ticket and securing diverse Cabinet and agency appointments. In particular, she wanted a woman to lead the Department of Health, Education, and Welfare (HEW) and a Native American as Secretary of the Interior.

Chisholm guaranteed many changes if she won the presidency. Once in office, she promised to hire African Americans at "all levels of government" to overhaul the way the administrative state worked. "If our federal programs are to do anything toward helping Blacks or any other minority," she said, "then those who develop and run them will need the insight and perspective and trust of minority people." Chisholm wanted to make the federal workforce more representative of and responsive to the people it served. "I run so that people who look like you and me can never again be taken for granted," she said.

Chisholm's candidacy began in earnest in Florida in 1972. Speaking to a Tampa audience in February, Chisholm called for unity among African Americans, women, and young people. "Join me on the Chisholm trail," she said, noting that together a unified front would better empower them to "participate in the decision-making process that governs all of our lives." With a shoestring budget, a team of volunteers, and a 21-year-old Cornell University student who earned both a salary and academic credit as her Florida campaign manager, Chisholm crisscrossed the state. She walked the picket line with striking sugarcane workers in Miami, speaking to them in fluent Spanish; she criticized George Wallace; and she challenged Black state leaders to back her. On Election Day, Chisholm finished seventh with 4 percent of the vote. Chisholm's policy positions highlighted the scope of her agenda. She called for the federal government to bolster its antipoverty efforts. She opposed the Vietnam War. She backed abortion rights. She supported a national health insurance. She welcomed the support of gay activists. She called for the legalization of marijuana and more.

Chisholm's Brooklyn district made urban affairs an important part of her campaign. She sought federal disaster relief for struggling cities and open housing policies to desegregate America. Chisholm also called for quality, universal public education and supported busing as "a legitimate temporary means to aid the integration of our public schools," noting the long history of Black children being bused and barred from white-only schools.

Even as Black political leaders criticized her campaign, Chisholm often remarked that it was more difficult for her to attract support as a woman in politics than as an African American. "What makes you think Black male politicians are any different from white male politicians?" she asked. Even allies in the women's movement hesitated to publicly support her outsider campaign. Bella Abzug, for instance, appeared at Chisholm's events but never officially endorsed her. Chisholm did receive the official backing of the Black Panther Party, which proclaimed that "every Black, poor, and progressive" person should vote for Chisholm.

Back home, Chisholm's Democratic competitors also criticized her presidential campaign. Thomas R. Fortune, a former Chisholm campaign staffer turned Democratic rival, suggested that Chisholm's national ambitions caused her to neglect the needs of her congressional district. "She was spending so much time with women's lib and gay lib that she was forgetting about Black lib right here in Bedford-Stuyvesant," Fortune said.

Throughout the spring primaries, Chisholm drew only a small percentage of the vote, but she frequently contended with accusations that she drew support from other candidates deemed more electable. Black leaders in North Carolina, for instance, warned that "a vote for Shirley Chisholm was a vote for George Wallace" that would undermine other white Democratic candidates sympathetic to African-American interests.

After losing California and New York, Chisholm returned home to campaign. She confessed to a Harlem audience that victory was unlikely but promised to be a "catalyst for change" at the convention. Chisholm remained confident that she could still be an "instrument of power" on the convention floor by convincing uncommitted delegates to support her.

Ultimately, however, Chisholm's strategy disintegrated as the Democratic National Convention approached. In late June, CBC members Walter Fauntroy of the District of Columbia, William Clay of Missouri, and Louis Stokes promised to deliver a bloc of Black delegates to put McGovern over the top and secure the nomination. When Chisholm arrived in Miami, she accused Black political leaders of having "sold out"

Black voters. Chisholm refused to back down and tried to use her small number of delegates —and persuasive skills—to block McGovern's path to the nomination.

Despite a last-minute maneuver by Humphrey and Chisholm it quickly became clear that McGovern had secured the nomination. That November, McGovern lost to Nixon in a landslide. Chisholm, meanwhile, retained her seat in the House, garnering nearly 88 percent of the vote in New York's Twelfth Congressional District.

Back in the House—where change was often a slow, grinding process—Chisholm remained determined to influence the policies and priorities of her party: seeking funding for job training programs, increasing pay for domestic workers, and broadly expanding antipoverty efforts. Like others in the CBC, she joined efforts to put economic pressure on South Africa's apartheid government.

Five years after running for president, Chisholm set her sights on winning the Democratic Caucus chair, the fourth-ranking elected office in party leadership at the time—and a position no woman had ever held. Again, Chisholm faced an uphill climb. "I don't think she ever actually asked anybody's permission to do anything," recalled Muriel Morisey, Chisholm's senior legislative assistant. "She was politically astute enough that she knew what was worth a fight." Running under the slogan, "Give Your Chair to a Lady," Chisholm had the support of the New York delegation, but ended up losing to the Agriculture Committee chair—and future Speaker of the House—Thomas S. Foley of Washington.

Despite the setback, Chisholm garnered two important positions in January 1977. She was elected secretary of the Democratic Caucus, where she helped set the party's agenda, and served in the position until 1981. She also became the first Black woman and only the second woman ever to sit on the powerful Rules Committee, which sets the terms of debate for every bill that reaches the House Floor but which required that she leave the Education and Labor Committee. Nevertheless, Chisholm explained that Rules gave her "much more clout," and enabled her to better support legislation "having to do with people who've been rather voiceless and powerless.

Although her presidential run came up short, Chisholm succeeded as a "catalyst for change" in American politics. Whether running for the White House or pursuing a seat on the influential House Rules Committee, Chisholm sought new and more powerful means to make the government both accountable to and representative of the American people.

For the Democrats, George Wallace obviously neither wanted nor expected Blacks to help him. Senator Edmund Muskie, early in his days as the Democratic front-runner, declared he would not take a Negro as a running mate. Senator George Mc Govern blazed through the primaries despite only scattered Negro support plus some late-blooming endorsements from Black leaders. And Hubert Humphrey, who jawed his way through the early primaries echoing George Wallace on the busing and welfare issues, received the lion's share of Black votes nonetheless.

To a large extent, the rise and fall of Black political power this year parallels the frustrating, sometimes poignant odyssey of U. S. Representative Shirley Chisholm, the first Black and the first woman ever to make a serious run at the Presidency of the United States.

But a decision could not be reached on whether to back Stokes, to adopt Bond's plan, or to throw in early with one of the white aspirants acceptable to Blacks. "This is very, very distressing to me," Shirley Chisholm told admirers at a Washington cocktail party last November. "As of this moment, the Black elected officials have not really come up with their strategy. Meanwhile, people are moving, and the essence is time. This is politics… In good conscience, I can't hold back."

A week earlier, in fact, Shirley Chisholm had made her intentions known to 1,300 supporters at the Americana Hotel in New York City: "I'm here to tell you tonight, yes, I dare to say I'm going to run for the Presidency… Other kinds of people can steer the ship of state besides white men… Regardless of the outcome, they will have to remember that a little hundred-pound woman, Shirley Chisholm, shook things up."

At first, her Black brothers in Congress merely ignored her. Asked about Mrs. Chisholm's budding candidacy, U. S. Representative Louis Stokes of Ohio, Carl's brother, simply shrugged and laughed, while Congressman Clay answered, "Who's Shirley Chisholm?"

Clay didn't have long to wait to find out. At a mid-November conference of Black elected officials, Mrs. Chisholm took the floor to verbally spank those who refused to take her seriously. "They're always plotting and planning for me," she raged, "but the Almighty God has borne me up. Shirley Chisholm is the highest elected Black woman official. You'd better wake up."

With outspoken defiance of convention, boundless energy and more than a little braggadocio, Shirley Chisholm thus leapfrogged the Black politicians and unilaterally cornered the market on black Presidential aspirations. The other leaders were embarrassed into sullen silence. "They were standing around, peeing on their shoes," snapped a Chisholm aide, "so Shirley finally said the hell with it and got a campaign going. If she hadn't, we'd still be without a Black candidate."

Julian Bond, for one, didn't agree. "She was absent from most discussions on strategy," Bond complained. "We may have been peeing on our shoes, but if we were, she wasn't around to get splashed."

Instead, Mrs. Chisholm took off on campaign swings through New York, Florida and California. She over flowed with enthusiasm, confidence and dedication to the proposition that she, more than any Black American, was best equipped to carry the banner for America's poor and disinfranchised. But these traits are not the stuff of which election victories are made; victory requires money, well-placed support and slick, professionally led political organization.

She began her campaign with little more than $40,000, a fraction of what other candidates would spend on TV commercials alone in the Florida primary. As for supporters, only Ronald Dellums of California came to her side early among her colleagues in the 13-member Black Caucus of the House of Representatives. Last January, a somewhat more reluctant endorsement was issued by Manhattan Borough President Percy Sutton. Mrs. Chisholm was quick to spread word of Sutton's endorsement among Black Floridians. Privately, she remained the icono clast:

"He described me as a fighter, courageous and all that s——," she fumed while jetting through Florida in January. "He could have done that two, three months ago and given me some momentum."

Local pros avoided her. In Georgia, State Senator Leroy Johnson quickly turned over his considerable Black organization in Atlanta to then front running Muskie. In Ohio, Louis Stokes sided with Humphrey as soon as Mrs. Chisholm had effectively cut the ground from under his brother Carl. In Florida, the first and most important test of Mrs. Chisholm's vote-getting power, Alcee Hastings, a Black Fort Lauderdale lawyer, also jumped to Muskie.

Hastings had run for the U. S. Senate in 1970, receiving 99,000 votes-17 per cent of the total in a state where Blacks made up fewer than 13 per cent of the 2.2 million registered Democrats. Under the Black political plan outlined by Julian Bond, Hastings would have run in the 1972 Florida Presidential primary as a favorite son. Once Mrs. Chisholm entered the race however, such a bid by Hastings would have made him look like Judas Iscariot. Indeed, any Black politician across the U.S. who dared to compete with her would be in a similar position.

She had no track record in Florida, Hastings observed. "The Black communities' political engineers already were with others... Had she been here earlier, or if she had enough money, she might have been able to overcome the problem. But this state is full of resident niggers hired by the white Public Relations people. You know what I mean. Like if I wanted to play the politics of morality, I would've been in the McGovern campaign... Blacks are like everybody else in politics — selfish, practical, political and playing the money game."

"Black politicians had more to gain for themselves as Humphrey's Black, or McGovern's Black, or Muskie's Black than as a strong but faceless coalition for Congresswoman Shirley Chisholm." Mrs. Chisholm encountered a Black leadership that was divided and occasionally hostile wherever she campaigned. In North Carolina, Black leaders went so far as to proclaim publicly that "a vote for Shirley Chisholm is a vote for George Wallace."

She was little better off in terms of political organization. Plans for a visit to Tampa were entrusted to Mrs. Dorothy Harmon, a Tampa teacher and ramrod for a proposed juvenile center. "Now, look," Mrs. Harmon warned newsmen covering the Chisholm tour, "we're not gonna promote this political stuff. She's here to publicize juvenile problems." Mrs. Harmon set aside 90 minutes of Mrs. Chisholm's time for a "rap session" with Tampa high school youths. Not one showed up, and Shirley Chisholm, alone and small, waited vainly in a parlor of Tampa's International Inn. Later, she spent an hour in a nearly deserted shopping center designed for Black-owned businesses. She met a total of eight potential voters, employees of the Boss Biddy, a fried-chicken emporium.

At the University of Miami, her staff was unable to find the political science class she was to address. They stumbled into a geography class with 29 students, and the young instructor prevailed on her to stay and talk for 15 minutes. Then she found the proper class of 100 students presided over by a Mr. Schecterman. "I'm an ex-Brooklynite," he proudly proclaimed. "From Bensonhurst. My wife's from Flatbush." Later, outside the Student Union, she drew a mere 200 students where two weeks earlier Muskie had attracted 2,000. It developed that most of the students happened on her quite by accident; there hadn't been a single poster or advertisement in the campus newspaper promoting her speech. And at what was to be a gala Miami rally, handled by a small group of white, chic liberationist young matrons and advertised as a $5-a-plate box-chicken supper, only 150 people showed up —and all they got was Mrs. Chisholm, Kool-Aid and store-bought cookies.

**As** a Black and a female, she is no stranger to the role of underdog. She owes the indefatigable self - confidence that carried her to Congress from the 12th District in New York largely to a firm but loving grandmother on the island of Barbados, where she spent most of her childhood. Her parents met in New York, after both left the Caribbean for the hoped-for pot of gold in the United States.

Although she was born in Brooklyn, November 30, 1924, Shirley St. Hill was deposited at the age of 3 with the grandmother, Mrs. Emaline Seale, along with two younger sisters (a fourth girl was later born to

60

the parents in New York). Emaline Seale, a straight backed, gray-haired woman, opened her farm home near Christ Church village not only to Shirley and two sisters, but to four other grandchildren. Among her daily chores, Shirley took sheep to pasture, milked cows and collected firewood. "Granny gave me strength, dignity and love," Mrs. Chisholm recalls. "I learned from an early age that I was somebody. I didn't need the Black revolution to teach me that."

She is an accomplished mimic; one of her best impressions is of Wilbur Mills, House Ways and Means Committee chairman, on their first encounter after her election to Congress: "'Er-ah, Missus Chisholm,' "she says, pushing her voice to its lowest register and affecting an Arkansas drawl, "'we, er-ah, want to welcome you, er-ah, to the Congress, but, my-my-my-my my-my, Missus Chisholm, we certainly hope you, er-ah, not gonna turn evahthing upside down heah.' "She concedes her colleagues may not take to her unorthodoxy, but she insists they admire her for it. "One of the members of the Black Caucus described me to one newsman this way," she, "'Shirley Chisholm is a pain in the ass. But she's a delightful pain in the ass.'"

When she was 13, the family moved to the Bedford Stuyvesant area of Brooklyn where she has lived, or maintained a residence, ever since. In those days, the neighborhood was changing from white to Black and she encountered her first racial hostility. ("The Jewish children would tell me their mothers had forbidden them to play with me.")

Later, at Brooklyn College, she first became aware of inequality of economic opportunity for Blacks. She decided to become a teacher ("What else could a Black woman do?") and developed a genuine fondness for children, though she had none of her own. Fortunately, later on in Mrs. Chisholm's life, she was able to have the opportunity to adopt a godson named Willie Kimmons. Ironically, the two had met briefly when he was a youngster in third grade in Memphis, Tennessee. Now she could continue to concentrate on her political career in pursuit to the 1972 Presidency. With all the mounting issues facing her as an African American and a female, Mrs. Chisholm was ready to pursue her political dream.

Her approach to issues reflects that same, frank blending of pragmatism and idealism. "We've got to get over reacting to labels emotionally," she told a Tallahassee audience in January. "What we've got to consider is: will it rebound to the benefit of people who are suffering?"

Now, as far as the term, "women's liberation" is concerned, marching on a picket line to open a bar that caters only to men—that's the middle-class white women's bag. It's not ours. But marching for national day-care centers, that's something else." Still, on the stump, Shirley Chisholm spends less time talking issues and most of her time talking Shirley Chisholm.

"They talk about my qualifications," she told more than 2,000 high school students in Miami. "'Shirley; they say, 'what qualifications do you have to presume to be President of the United States?' Well, I have a near-genius I.Q...if that means anything. I have four college degrees, if that means anything. I am 10 credits from a PhD., if that means anything. I'm the only candidate that speaks Spanish fluently...what else do you want? With near messianic fervor. **Including bachelor's and master's degrees and two education certificates for additional graduate work.** Mrs. Chisholm exhorted her audiences to take her seriously—and she sensed early in her campaign that Blacks would be as difficult to convince as whites: "I want to be the candidate for those who see beyond my Blackness and femaleness and see a candidate who has ability, guts, leadership, talent, honesty, sincerity and who refuses to indulge in sham and hypocrisy... If you look at the qualifications of the Presidents of the United States of America, you'd have to say that Shirley Chisholm is up with the top five...

"I need you to get back to your mothers and fathers and your grandmothers and grand fathers who are so conditioned to believe that only a white man can be President, to say, 'Mom, dad, let's give the sister a chance for once.' They feel so inferior about themselves they would rather go out there and vote for a white. Here's the opportunity for once to reverse the tables. Come with me. Just once."

Despite her bombast, Shirley Chisholm, by her own admission, is a creature of the American Dream. She believes in the system. She campaigned long and hard to make it work for her—walking the ghetto streets, shaking hands in bars and pool halls, making the campus and banquet circuits, visiting day care centers, being interviewed at every opportunity. "The American Dream can become an actuality and a reality," she told one audience. She said if she could control 50 delegates, she could bargain with the front-runners in a deadlocked convention. (It is estimated that she could get as many as 100 votes on the first ballot if, as expected, some uncommitted Black delegates vote for her.) "I don't have money," she said during a recent television interview. "I don't have endorsers. But I'm still trudging along.... We're going to be in for a great lot of eye-opening at that convention.

**S**he has said she would demand a Black on the ticket, a woman to head the Department of Health, Education and Welfare, and an Indian to run the Department of the Interior. "I am not backed by fat cats or the corporate interests of this country ... We can turn things around in 1972 if we put it together. I am your instrument," she says, her hands extended palms upward and her voice rising dramatically. "I am your instrument for change. Give your vote to me instead of one of those warmed-over gentlemen who come to you once every four years. Give your vote to me. I belong to you."

Wherever she was able to draw a crowd, rank-and-file Blacks responded enthusiastically—and many Black leaders were induced to give her implied support. But it proved to be mostly polite sham. "She's getting the rah-rah treatment," observed Bill Oates, Black owner of a prospering restaurant in Tallahassee. "But when it comes to getting out and voting and raising money, everybody will sit on their behinds."

Black male antipathy toward Mrs. Chisholm may well have been heightened by concern that enthusiastic support for a Black woman would be taken as proof of the theory that Negroes form a matriarchal subculture within American society — a theory that most Black intellectuals have hotly rejected. For her part, Mrs. Chisholm explains it as plain male chauvinism. Asked why her Black Congressional colleagues were cool to her candidacy, she replied: "What makes you think Black male politicians are any different from white male politicians? ...This 'woman thing' is so deep. I've found it out in this campaign. I never knew it before."

How can you call meetings and make agendas when you know you're in somebody's pocket? People say to me, 'Chizzy, you can't make it ... Your own people are hurting you.' But I say to you, my brothers and sisters, if you cannot help me, don't hurt me. Keep quiet."

"You know, everybody goes through so much to get this most important position—the press men, the buses, the signs, the staff men running back and forth. And there I sit with my little crew, knowing that I'm the only unique candidate out there, thinking in the depths of my heart that I might be the one to decide the nominee ... I'm very serious with what I'm doing in this country … If we want change in America, we can't get it by sitting back and letting the traditional things happen." Congresswoman Shirley Chisholm's road to the Presidency has been extremely difficult, painful and time consuming. She has endured personal threats and humiliation from Black male and white male elected officials, some whom she supported for office.

The years of 1968 and 1972 were a pivotal point in her personal and political life. As a result of these brutal undertakings, Mrs. Chisholm learned a great deal about people of all races and sexes. The best training she had was from her grandmother Emaline Seale, while living in Barbados on their farm. She was relentless in her pursuit of the Presidency. Even though she knew her chances of winning in 1972 were slim to none. Her main intent was to raise the awareness level of African Americans, especially women, that by the Grace of God and hard work, anything is possible. If you don't make a concerted effort, and are not at the table, where the real political decisions are being made, you don't have a voice and it will be difficult to succeed.

# CHAPTER 7

# SHIRLEY CHISHOLM'S TRANSITION FROM POLITICS TO EDUCATIONAL CONSULTING, COLLEGE PROFESSOR, COMMUNITY LEADER AND PUBLIC SERVANT

*Mrs. Chisholm and me*

After retiring from Congress in 1983, Mrs. Chisholm was popular on the lecture circuit. She was the co-founder of the Unity Democratic Club in Brooklyn, New York. Shirley Chisholm was one of the early members of the National Organization of Women (NOW) and active in the National Association for the Advancement of Colored People (NAACP). In 1993, she was inducted into the National Women's Hall of Fame.

From 1983 to 1987, Shirley Chisholm served as a Purington Professor at Mount Holyoke College, the oldest women's college in Massachusetts, where she taught politics and women's studies. In 1985, she was a visiting scholar at Spelman College in Atlanta, Georgia and Rutgers University in New Brunswick, New Jersey. She was also a guest speaker at Daytona Beach Community College, in Daytona Beach, Florida; Jacksonville Community College in Jacksonville, Florida and countless numbers of public schools, 2 and 4-year colleges and universities in this country. Mrs. Chisholm did a number of television and radio interviews, discussing the issues of gender bias, education, civil rights and politics. She worked on the Presidential campaign of Rev. Jesse Jackson and announced his candidacy for the Presidency in 1984 in Washington, DC. Mrs. Chisholm also served as graduation speaker, visiting professor and lecturer for me, her adopted godson, Dr. Willie Kimmons as The Shirley Chisholm Educational Institute at the University of the District of Columbia (UDC) in 1983 and 1984 in Washington, DC.

I kept Congresswoman Chisholm involved by inviting her to be my graduation speaker and Summer Institute Presenter at colleges and universities where I was employed as a dean, vice president, president and chancellor.

Listed are the educational institutions I invited Mrs. Chisholm to speak and make presentations:

1.  St. Francis College in Brooklyn, New York where I served as Dean of Adult, Continuing Education and Community Services, 1977, 1978,1979.
2.  Wayne County Community College in Detroit, Michigan, where I was President of the Downtown Campus, 1979, 1980, 1981, 1982, 1983.
3.  University of the District of Columbia where I was Dean of the College of Education and Human Ecology, Washington, DC., 1983, 1984, 1985.
4.  Fayetteville State University in Fayetteville, North Carolina where I was Dean of the School of Education, 1986, 1987, 1988.
5.  Gaston College in Gastonia, North Carolina where I was Dean of Liberal Arts & Sciences, 1989, 1990, 1991.
6.  Lawson State Community College in Birmingham, Alabama where I was Vice President for Academic and Student Affairs, 1992 -1994, 1997, 1998.

*Mrs. Chisholm received the bust of herself done by one of the art students when I, her godson, served as Vice President for Academic and Student Affairs at Lawson State Community College in Birmingham, Alabama. She served as the Commencement Speaker in 1993.*

*The Honorable Congresswoman, Shirley Chisholm was the graduation*
*speaker at Ivy Tech Community College, Bloomington, Indiana in 2000,*
*where I, her godson, served as the founding Chancellor of the College.*

7.  Trenholm Community College in Montgomery, Alabama where
    I was President, 1995, 1996.
8.  Ivy Tech Community College in Bloomington, Indiana where
    I served as the founding Chancellor of the College, 1999, 2000,
    2001.

"Mrs. C", as I called her, would tease me, by saying, "Willie, every time
you invite me to speak, you are working at a different college or university."
My immediate response was, "Mrs. C, you instilled in me through the
years, to be a risk-taker, a change-agent and to always explore my career
options." Therefore, I kept moving around the country and kept getting
promotions from Black and white colleges and universities. I went from
assistant dean to dean to vice president, president and chancellor.

At each of these educational institutions, I initiated a summer lecture
series in her name as, "The Shirley Chisholm Institute". I would always
have two open sessions at the college or university for the community
as a "Public Community Forum". She kept an extremely busy schedule
which eased her mind after so many tragic situations. Even when she left
Williamsville, New York in 1991 and moved to Palm Coast, Florida, near
Daytona Beach, Florida where I had retired, I kept her involved. Once
again, she spoke at educational and civic groups. These included Chambers
of Commerce, sororities, Bethune Cookman University in Daytona Beach,

churches, youth groups and many other organizations including the local NAACP.

Shirley Chisholm realized through her life of leadership and fighting against gender bias and racism that Black and brown women are the backbone of our communities. Throughout the course of our nation's history, Black and brown women have saved America's credibility and democracy. Shirley Chisholm authored two books during her lifetime: "Unbought and Unbossed" (1970), which became her campaign slogan and "The Good Fight", (1973). She addressed 8 crucial areas Black Americans should always use and know as our priorities in life:

1) Praising God daily
2) Economic Development
3) Civic and Community Engagement
4) Criminal Justice Issues
5) Education Issues
6) Health Care Disparity
7) Voting Rights
8) Gender Bias

Mrs. Chisholm's long-time missions in life as an educator, public servant, community leader and politician were to ensure the protection of rights of all persons. Her constant political commitment was to address social justice, economic equality, racial hatred, gender bias, and Black on Black crimes.

Some of Congresswoman Chisholm's favorite quotes were:

"I am and always will be a "catalyst of change".

"When morality comes up against profit, it is seldom that profit loses".

"We have to study and analyze ourselves as opposed to being studied and analyzed by others".

"If they don't give you a seat at the table, bring a folding chair."

"The emotional, sexual and psychological stereotyping of females begins when the doctor says, 'It's a girl'".

"Service is the rent we pay for the privilege of living on this earth."

"You don't make progress by standing on the sidelines, whimpering and complaining. You make progress by implementing ideas."

"Laugh when you can, apologize when you should, and let go what you can't change. Kiss slowly, play hard, forgive quickly, take chances, give everything and have no regrets. Life is too short to be anything but happy".

"Racism is so universal in this country, so widespread and deep-seated, that it is invisible because it is so normal."

"We must reject not only the stereotypes that others hold of us, but also the stereotypes that we hold of ourselves."

"Success is no accident. It is hard work, perseverance, learning, studying, sacrifice and most of all, love of what you are doing or learning to do."

Mrs. Chisholm stated, *"Black male politicians are no different from white male politicians. This woman thing is so deep. I found it out in my 1972 campaign when I ran for President. This is something I never knew before."*

When Congresswoman Chisholm decided not to seek re-election, she cited her long-standing intention never to remain in politics throughout her productive and creative life. She revealed the frustration and difficulty of serving her constituents while conservatives control government in Washington, DC. Also, because of the traffic accident that her second husband, Art Hardwick, was involved in, she needed time to assist him with his long road to recovery. In addition, she would spend time writing, teaching, lecturing, traveling around the world and spending time with her adopted godson, Willie, attending a social event in Daytona Beach, Florida.

She hoped during her retirement years to create a new national state of mind that demands peace, prosperity and equality for all Americans.

Former Congresswoman, Shirley Chisholm, further stated that when she observed what's happening through mass media and throughout our neighborhoods, cities, counties and country, she was compelled to give her opinion. As a race of people, we have to start now to make a concerted effort to orientate and educate African Americans and people of color on the importance of being a registered voter and vote. Voting is and should be one of our most important priorities.

During her run for President in 1972, Shirley Chisholm pushed a platform focused on racial and gender equity, elevating those issues to the national stage. She also adopted yellow and purple as her campaign colors, inspiring future female politicians, including Vice President Kamala Harris to wear purple in her honor. Former President Bill Clinton in 1993 approached Shirley Chisholm with what he thought would be a great opportunity for her to be the next Ambassador to Jamaica. But Mrs. Chisholm gave the former President two responses, 1) her professional response and 2) her personal response. She stated in her eloquent, strong and elaborate tone, "Mr. President, thanks for the opportunity to serve my people because I have strong ties with many people in the islands, especially Barbados and Jamaica. But you have reduced the operating budget in Jamaica, and my Jamaican friends would have great expectations of me to improve their country's life style and situation. My personal and political reputation would be damaged severely, something I have spent a lifetime developing. I'm sorry, but I will not be able to undertake such an assignment under those circumstances. Now, my public response is, because of health-related issues, I'm unable to pursue this wonderful offer presented to me by President Bill Clinton. Thanks for thinking of me."

Former Congresswoman Shirley Chisholm's transition from politics to her private community and public life was a rather well-planned transition. She always stated that politicians should serve no more than 15 to 20 years. Once you pass the 15-year mark, one began to become irrelevant, bored, complacent and repetitive in their work for people. If you haven't made an impact by the 15th year, you begin to lose your interest and the real ability to serve with stamina, commitment and integrity. It is time to make a concerted effort to move on and pass the torch to someone else. This is one of the biggest problems with politicians, they stay too long and refuse to allow or recruit others to come into the political arena.

With this mentality of politicians, serving the people becomes secondary to serving themselves. I always said once I thoroughly learned the political process and lifestyle, I realized that for most politicians, politics is for people who do not want to make an honest living. The work becomes a constant state of repetitiveness and self-serving and very little, if anything, gets done. We spent an enormous amount of time fighting within and between the parties and the constituents they served. The communities always suffers.

Today, we have too many politicians making a life-long living out of politics, 30, 40, 50 years and more. The technology and mass media are moving so fast today that after 10 or 25 years of serving, most things, ideas, decisions, needs and wants of the people have made a tremendous change in our society.

Also, the term limits for Congress politicians should be adjusted from a 2-year cycle to a 2 six-year cycle. Because a 2-year cycle politician spends his or her time constantly campaigning to get re-elected. The Congress person's time limit should coincide with the 6-year term of the senatorial position.

When politicians become complacent, very little time is spent on the work to be done in one's district they are serving. Too many years of serving the people beyond 15 years, one begins to think that they are the only one who can serve and they own the political position. This is where we lose a great deal of young, bright minded people who are willing and ready to serve and committed to bringing in fresh and new ideas, as well as, new energy. This is a commitment that Mrs. Chisholm made when she was elected in 1968 as the first Black U.S. Congresswoman to be elected, a 15-year limit to serve the people. Hopefully, someone in the political arena will introduce a bill and get it approved by both parties to only have two six-year terms for Congressional seats and Senatorial seats. In my opinion, this would eliminate all the parties' control and gridlocks when it comes to real and meaningful decision-making for the people they serve.

Mrs. Chisholm was great, very smart, courageous, and a visionary leader. She demonstrated through the years that she has done outstanding things as a Black woman. It has been documented that she was successful in her struggle for women's rights, especially for Black and brown women.

The unique thing about Mrs. Chisholm was her commitment to her people, Black, brown folks and especially women. She would say to me, "Willie, my son, politics is about 3 things: 'horse trading', 'I O U's' and 'longevity' and most Black politicians don't understand this. That's why we, as Black politicians, will never be in a place to make real decisions." She would also state to me, "Willie, I've come to realize that politics is for people who do not want to make an honest living. These were some of the reasons, after 7 terms as a Congresswoman, I knew I had to leave politics altogether. When I first came to Congress after being elected in 1968, my goal was to stay only 8 to 10 years because of the political landscape. There were mostly white males holding down all the most powerful and important committees. It would be a long time before Black and brown people, especially women, could garner enough support to remove the old, gray- haired, white men out of their powerful committee chair positions."

This brief narrative of the late, great, Shirley Chisholm's life and legacy was an abbreviated version of a remarkable human being's contribution to society. The narrative covered many crucial and personal events of Mrs. Chisholm's personal and professional life. Mrs. "C", as I called her, continued to go to the extreme to protect her private life. Unfortunately, there were very few people she trusted. Therefore, she lived her life in total secrecy as a loner.

*Mrs. Chisholm and me, her adopted godson, Willie.*

# CHAPTER 8

# SUMMARY OF HER POLITICAL CAREER AND THE LATER YEARS OF THE FORMER CONGRESSWOMAN SHIRLEY CHISHOLM'S LIFE

The life and legacy of the Honorable Shirley Anita St. Hill Chisholm-Hardwick's life is a true testimony of the love, hard work, commitment, pain, and suffering of an unusually strong and proud African American woman. She was one who defied all the odds, hurdles and constraints that this sexist and racist system put in her path. Due to the strict disciplinary up bringing she acquired from her beloved father and her grandmother, Shirley Anita St. Hill developed a tenacity not only to survive but become a genuine leader who understood her rich history. She was an eager learner who was well disciplined and extremely gifted in education, speaking ability and leadership skills. Her father and grandmother instilled in her early on in her life, that she could be anything she wanted to be in this world. Always study hard, read everything you could and have a strong belief and faith in God! If Mrs. Chisholm were alive today, I'm sure she would be extremely disappointed in the lack of progress African Americans have made in this country, especially in the areas of education, race relations, criminal justice, affordable housing, jobs, and Black on Black crime.

She would be delighted to know the progress made by one of the many organizations she helped to create as co-founder with Dr. C. Delores Tucker. The National Political Congress of Black Women in 1984 had made tremendous strides in getting more Black, brown and white women in elected political offices at the local, district, regional and national levels. She was the recipient of numerous Honorary Doctorate degrees from Black and white colleges and universities.

Former Congresswoman Chisholm concluded that racism, sexism, gender bias, poverty and the Vietnam War were all interrelated and equally wrong in depriving Black, brown people and the nation of its vitality. As she would often say to me during our educational and political sessions at her home in Florida, "A constructive, useful life, good works and good relationships are as valid as writing poetry or inventing a machine. Anything that one does well and obtains satisfaction from is a good enough reason for living. To be a decent human being that people like and feel better for knowing is enough. These are some of the traits Shirley Chisholm built her life around.

When I think of all the political maneuvering, racist tactics, gender bias that Congresswoman Shirley Chisholm endured, I often think of the sayings of Dr. Jack Levine, founder of the 4 Generations Institute in Tallahassee, Florida -April 28, 2021 in his article titled, "Counteracting Negativity-we can all take responsibility". Here I'll paraphrase his comments...

- "We all need a vision of hope to meet challenges and accept responsibility for making a difference for ourselves, our families and in whatever personal pursuit we choose to exercise with our positive energy.
- In advocacy work, one has the honor to meet a good number of impressive people at all stages of life who dedicate themselves to the betterment of others, like the Honorable Shirley Chisholm.
- While people's backgrounds are diverse and their activities take different roads to a common goal, realize one thing is constant.... those who care deeply are motivated by a great imagination for achievement. Mrs. Chisholm lived her political and personal life like this.
- In Proverbs 29:18 we read "Where there is no vision, the people perish." As the child of a blind father, one learns at a young age that there's a difference between sight and vision.
- Eyesight gives us the capacity to observe daily life in its vivid detail and varied dimension. Vision is the ability to see what could be. When we put ourselves in the position to envision a world where love for others and justice prevails, our actions can follow.
- Like the veteran at the window, let's pledge to take the opportunity to inspire others, no matter the odds and even in the face of negativity, as Congresswoman Shirley Chisholm did numerous

times during her political career facing great opposition from white and Black males and sometimes women.

- Always make a commitment to ourselves and others who need us because that provides us the power to leave a lasting legacy.

- Despite the good works performed by so many dedicated colleagues, we must admit that there is a great degree of negativity and stress-provoking anger around us.

- Just as road rage is frightful and dangerous, in some ways, vocal rage is a form of violence and is similarly perilous.

- Abusive language spewing from anyone's mouth is an embarrassment. Words matter and if we don't find a way to limit the vitriol, we will doubtless suffer dire consequences. Mrs. Chisholm endured a tremendous amount of criticism, jealousy, racism and vulgar language during her political and private life. In spite of it all, she stayed focused and continued to succeed in defying all the odds.

- Therefore, with pronouncements which divide us by enflaming animosities, pitting one against another, magnifying differences rather than celebrating our diversities, creates a setting for hatred to thrive. Shirley Chisholm addressed and confronted this with professional class and pride in spite of all the negativity.

- Strive to have an advocate role to dissuade anyone who sets a bad example for our children. The trauma of abuse and neglect in any form can have lifelong impact.

- Always try to encourage people to find common ground and stimulate civil conversation to reach mutual goals…across the generations.

- We are aware that many of us are blessed to enjoy positive emotional connections with family members, friends, mentors and role models who help us see the brighter side of life. But sadly, too many others are just out there, living with the insanity of hate. This is something Mrs. Chisholm fought against all of her life.

- Because unchecked hate can infect over time until it poisons the atmosphere and damages anyone in its pernicious path; it's time to defuse the insults, confront the hatred, and elevate the tone and tenor in our homes, communities, nation and worldwide…in both personal and political discourse. Mrs. Chisholm was confronted with this behavior all of her personal and political life.

- We need to hear more about solutions. How do we cure the sick body and souls of millions—young and old? Certainly not by ignoring their problems or excluding them from the opportunities of a positive society.

- We should try, every day, to help those whose paths we cross to be a symbol of hope not fear, and understanding not disenchantment. Hopefully, people can share the belief that we are keepers of our fellow travelers.

- This life is not just about us; it should be about the people we are serving as a public official. We are all dependent on someone else. The day we arrived on the planet, someone else did the work, God first—we just showed up. Together, we must keep the faith and share wisdom and understanding for people who are not as fortunate as we are.

- We should enjoy keeping in touch as we look forward to our next level of achievements for the children and family members of all ages in our communities that we serve as public servants and political leaders. Because our children are an extension of us, our children are our greatest resource and our children are our future."

- Mrs. Chisholm stated that she wanted to be remembered as a person who lived in the 20th century and dared to be a catalyst for change. I remember her saying to me, "*Willie, many of our Black and brown sisters and brothers are too complacent. You be a risk-taker and a change-agent and make things happen in life.*" "It's been a joy and great pleasure for me to highlight some of the special moments during my lifetime that I spent with a wonderful human being labeled as my adopted godmother."

The purpose of this brief narrative is to highlight Mrs. Chisholm's life and legacy and to maintain her relevancy and contributions to society. It is also to give another view point of the life of a brave and visionary fighter who had a strong will not only to survive, but to be successful against all odds. This hopefully would serve as a model and testament to all Black and brown people, especially Black and brown women and women of all colors and races. Mrs. Chisholm's life and legacy should be a road map for Black and brown people in the future to strive for because she would say, *"Through faith, everything is possible for those who believe."*

My mother, Mrs. Annie
Florence Kimmons-Jones

My godmother, Mrs.
Shirley Anita St. Hill
Chisholm - Hardwick

Finally, this book on the personal, private, professional, political life and legacy of my adopted godmother, Mrs. Shirley Chisholm, has been an opportunity to say thanks. Mrs. Chisholm and my mother, Mrs. Annie Kimmons-Jones, inspired and encouraged me to become a strong, self-sufficient, independent Black male.

My adopted godmother, Mrs. Shirley Anita St. Hill Chisholm-Hardwick and my biological mother, Mrs. Annie Florence Kimmons-Jones had a long history of friendship. The two of them met years ago in Memphis, Tennessee. Later on, they developed a friendship and discussed me often as I grew from a young 9-year-old boy into adulthood. My mother would visit me often as I was employed as an administrator at different colleges and universities. She made many trips from Memphis to Washington, D.C. where I was Dean of the College of Education at the University of the District of Columbia while Mrs. Chisholm was in Congress. The three of us often had lunch during my mother's visits to Washington, D.C. As a young male, I was blessed to have a godmother and mother in my life. Thank God for them both.

Mrs. Shirley Chisholm has been a tremendous impact on my life. During our special time of reading and many lengthy educational and political conversations, she enjoyed citing the quote entitled, "Love to Live", authors unknown. Her special personal quote was, "a Message for Life and Living". It was ironic because she read these two sayings after her 80th birthday on November 30, 2004. Shirley Chisholm passed away peacefully on January 1, 2005, some 31 days later. I have attached her two quotes for your reading pleasure. Enjoy the reading.

God bless my mother and my godmother, Willie

My godmother's two favorite poems:

## LOVE TO LIVE

Today dear Lord I'm 80 and there is so much I haven't done.
I hope dear Lord, you'll let me live until I'm 81.
But then if I haven't finished all I want to do, would you please let me stay awhile until I'm 82? So many places I want to go, so very much to see. Do you think that I could manage to make it to 83?

The world is changing very fast there is so much more in store. I'd like it very much to live until I'm 84. And if by then I'm still alive, I'd like to stay 'til 85. More planes will be in the air so I would like to stick around and see what happens to the world when I turn 86.

I know dear Lord, it's much to ask and it must be nice in Heaven, but I'd really like to stay here until I'm 87. I know by then I won't be fast and sometimes I'll be late, but it would be so pleasant to be here at 88.

I will have seen so many things and had a wonderful time, so I'm sure that I'd be willing to leave when I'm 89.

Just one more thing I'd like to say Dear Lord, I thank you kindly, but if it's okay with you I'd love to live past 90. ---Author Unknown

## A MESSAGE FOR LIFE AND LIVING

ALWAYS GIVE HONOR AND PRAISE TO GOD, OUR SUPREME BEING FOR THIS WONDERFUL DAY. BECAUSE GOD IS GOOD ALL THE TIME AND ALL THE TIME GOD IS GOOD. GOD IS AN AWESOME GOD.
JUST TRY HIM.

THANK GOD FOR WAKING US THIS MORNING IN OUR RIGHT FRAME OF MIND.
SO, WITH IMAGINATION, INGENUITY AND AUDACITY, EXPLORE, DISCOVERY, CHANGE THE WORLD.
AND HAVE FUN WHILE YOU'RE AT IT.
ALWAYS TAKE TIME OUT TO LOVE AND TO LIVE.
YOU'RE GOING TO BE BUSY, BUT NEVER FORGET GOD, FAMILY AND FRIENDS.
HAVE REGULAR HOURS FOR WORK AND PLAY.
MAKE EACH DAY BOTH USEFUL AND PLEASANT AND PROVE THAT YOU UNDERSTAND THE WORTH OF TIME BY EMPLOYING IT WELL; THEN YOUTH WILL BE DELIGHTFUL, OLD AGE WILL BRING FEW REGRETS AND LIFE WILL BECOME A BEAUTIFUL SUCCESS.

BECAUSE LIFE IS VERY FRAGILE AND EXTREMELY SHORT AND TOMORROW ISN'T PROMISED.

OPPORTUNITIES ARE LIKE SURPRISES. IF YOU WAIT TOO LONG,
YOU WILL MISS THEM.                    ---------Author Unknown

FINALLY, SHE WOULD ASK FOR GOD'S BLESSINGS DURING THE STRUGGLES OF LIFE.

This brief narrative of Shirley Chisholm's life and legacy for me has been a work of love, commitment and dedication. I thank God for bringing me into her life as an adopted godson.

*God bless your soul and rest in peace, godmother.*

*Dr. Willie J. Greer Kimmons, Educational Consultant for Pre K-16 Schools; Title I Schools, Teachers and Parents; Motivational Speaker; Author; Former Classroom Teacher, College Professor, College President, Chancellor, Military Officer, Public Servant and Community Leader, Founder, President/CEO, Save Children Save Schools, Inc. 1653 Lawrence Circle, Daytona Beach, FL 32117*

*Office: (386) 253-4920*
*Cell: (386)451-4780 www.savechildrensaveschools.com.*
*wjkimmons@aol.com*

# AFTERWORD

By Dr. John Ed Mathison

It's good when we can be introduced to some people who are trailblazers in providing many of the opportunities we have today. From my history of political figures, especially African-American women, the Honorable Shirley Chisholm was one of those trailblazers. She did many great things for women in civil and human rights. Her life was difficult and stressful, but she survived it and did what she believed. In the long run, that's what truly matters. I salute a woman who was always setting goals and accomplishing them.

Shirley Chisholm had a commitment to quality as a teacher in the classroom, a community leader, a public servant, a career politician, or a motivational speaker. She was a person who was always a catalyst for change. That's how she earned the nickname "Fighting Shirley". I was especially impressed that Congresswoman Chisholm was a person who would always look to God for ultimate approval, and not to man. She believed looking to man for approval would always be mixed up and twisted. Focusing on a strong faith in God in everything that you do will always see you through any situation.

Shirley Chisholm is the woman who paved the way, laid the foundation and raised the awareness level for Hillary Clinton, Barack Obama, and Kamala Harris, and hundreds of black, brown, and white female elected officials in this country. Every woman owes her a great deal of gratitude.

I am making the best effort possible to be a community leader from a Christian perspective. My life's work is dedicated on many of the principles that Honorable Shirley Chisholm advocated. Through my leadership ministries, vision is one of hope, inspiration, challenges and love. I'm inspired in reading how Ms. Chisholm built her life around these same principles. It was her tremendous contribution that made me excited about writing the afterword for her godson, Dr. Willie J. Greer Kimmons' book about the Life and Legacy of Shirley Anita St. Hill Chisholm-Hardwick. It is my prayer that you will put into practice in our lives these valuable qualities that Congresswoman Chisholm espoused.


Dr. John Ed Mathison of Montgomery, Alabama. Pastor Emeritus retired after serving 36 years as senior minister of Frazer Memorial United Methodist Church in Montgomery, Alabama. He is the author of 11 books and writes a weekly blog for newspapers on religious life and community-related issues.

# BOOKS BY THE HONORABLE
# SHIRLEY CHISHOLM

Chisholm, Shirley (1970). <u>Unbought Unbossed:</u> An Autobiography, Boston, Massachusetts, Houghton Mifflin Harcourt Publishing Company.

Chisholm, Shirley (1973). <u>The Good Fight:</u> (A Cass Canfield Book). New York, New York, Harper Collins Publishers.

# BIBLIOGRAPHY

"A Divided Nation Fights for Freedom": (2016), the National Museum of African American History and Culture, Chapter 3, Section 6, The Great Debates between President Abraham Lincoln and Abolitionist Frederick Douglass, Washington, D.C.

Brownmiller, Susan. Shirley Chisholm: (1971). A Biography. Doubleday, Garden City, New York.

Burnett-Rosalind Jones – March 7, 2021, email stated that slave Reverend William Rush-Plummer was her great-grandfather.

"Catalyst for Change": (1972). The Presidential Campaign of Representative Shirley Chisholm. Ebony and Jet Magazine Interview. Chicago, Illinois.

"Catalyst for Change": The 1972 Presidential Campaign of Representative Shirley Chisholm-US House of Representatives History Office of Art and Archives and Office of the Historian, Washington, DC.

"Catalyst for Change": The 1972 Presidential Campaign of Representative Shirley Chisholm-Women and Minorities on the Hill and Members of Congress, Congressional Black Caucus Publication, Washington, DC.

Chisholm, Shirley (1970). Unbought Unbossed: An Autobiography, Houghton Mifflin Harcourt Publishing Company, Boston, Massachusetts.

Chisholm, Shirley (1973). The Good Fight: (A Cass Canfield Book). Harper Collins Publishers, New York, New York.

Drotning, Phillip T., and Wesley W. South (1970). Up from the Ghetto. Cowles Book Company, New York, New York.

Duffy, Susan, comp. (1998). Shirley Chisholm: A Bibliography of Writings by and about her. Scarecrow Press, Metuchen, New Jersey.

Ebony Jet Magazine (1969). Recorded interview of Mrs. Chisholm. Chicago, Illinois.

Excerpts from Mrs. Chisholm's speech at Howard University, by Laura W. Murphy, April 21, 1969, Washington, D.C.

Excerpts from a speech by Mrs. Chisholm, "The Black Woman in Contemporary America", June 17, 1974, University of Missouri, Kansas City, Missouri.

Gallagher, Julie, (2007). Waging "The Good Fight": The Political Career of Shirley Chisholm, 1953-82," The Journal of African American History 92:3, 393.

Gillespie, Janet, An Abridged version, "What to the Slave is the Fourth of July 5, 1852 Speech", by Frederick Douglass, Rochester, New York. December 28, 2021

Jones-Beatrice Plummer, March 7, 2021. Email stated slave Reverend William Rush-Plummer was her grandfather.

Kimmons, Willie J., (1977). Black Administrators in Public Community Colleges, Self-perceived Role and Status: A Hearthstone Book, Carlton Press, Inc., New York, N. Y.

Kimmons, Willie J. and Mims, George (1980). The Minority Administrator in Higher Education: Progress, Experiences and Perspectives. Schenkman Publishing Company, Cambridge, Massachusetts

Kimmons, Willie J. Greer (2012), A Parenting Guidebook: The roles of school, family, teachers, religion, politics, community, local, state and federal government in assisting parents with rearing their children., Author House Publishing Company, Bloomington, Indiana.

Kimmons, Willie J. Greer (2016), The Making of an Urban Community College in a Union and Political Environment:  A Historical Perspective of Wayne County Community College, Detroit, Michigan, 1964-2016. Author House Publishing Company, Bloomington, Indiana.

Kimmons, Willie J. and Ingraham, Gayle S. (2021). <u>Parenting Forever Workbook,</u> Author House Publishing Company, Bloomington, Indiana

Kimmons, Willie J. (2022). <u>The Personal, Private, Professional, Political Life and Legacy of the Honorable Shirley Anita St. Hill Chisholm-Hardwick,</u> Author House Publishing Company, Bloomington, Indiana.

Kunjufu, Jawanza (1991). <u>"Black Economics":</u> Solutions for Economic and Community Empowerment. African American Images, Chicago, Illinois.

Lesher, Stephan (June 25, 1972). "<u>The Short, Unhappy Life of Black of Presidential Politics</u>", The New York Times, New York, NY.

Levine, Jack (April 28, 2021). "<u>Counteracting Negativity, we can all take responsibility."</u> 4 Generations Institute, Tallahassee, Florida.

Maddens, Richard L. (January 29,1969 p.16) "<u>Mrs. Chisholm Gets Off House Farm Committee",</u> The New York Times, New York, NY.

Proctor, Samuel DeWitt, (1995). <u>The Substance of Things Hoped For</u>", Memoir of African-American Faith. G.P. Putnam's Sons. New York, New York.

Rennert, Richard Scott, ed.(1993) <u>Female Leaders.</u>: Chelsea House, Publishers, New York, New York.

Scheader, Catherine (1990). <u>Shirley Chisholm: Teacher and Congresswoman.</u> Hillsdale, N. J.:Enslow,

Stories from the People's House, Shirley Chisholm (2018). <u>House of Representatives</u>, Washington, DC, Women and Minorities on Capitol Hill.

Whereas: <u>Stories from The People's House,</u> Blog, OHH-Blog, September 14, 2020. "Catalyst for Change": The1972 Presidential Campaign of Representative Shirley Chisholm.

Wikipedia, The Free Encyclopedia, Shirley Chisholm, May 14, 2021.

Wikipedia, The Free Encyclopedia, Harriet Tubman, November 26, 2007.

Wikipedia, The Free Encyclopedia, Fannie Lou Hamer, August 2, 2021.

Wikipedia, The Free Encyclopedia, Sojourner Truth, August 3, 2021.

Wikipedia, The Free Encyclopedia, William Rush-Plummer, December 26, 2020.

Woodson, Carter G. (1933), <u>"The Mis-education of the Negro"</u>: The Associated Publishers, Inc. 1407 14<sup>th</sup> Street, N.W., Washington, D.C.

Printed in the United States
by Baker & Taylor Publisher Services